C000142102

SHORT

INTRODUCTIONS TO FILM STUDIES

OTHER TITLES IN THE SHORT CUTS SERIES

THE SPORTS FILM

GAMES PEOPLE PLAY

BRUCE BABINGTON

WALLFLOWER

LONDON and NEW YORK

A Wallflower Press Book
Published by
Columbia University Press
Publishers Since 1893
New York • Chichester, West Sussex
cup.columbia.edu

Copyright © Bruce Babington 2014
All rights reserved.
Wallflower Press® is a registered trademark of Columbia University Press.

A complete CIP record is available from the Library of Congress

ISBN 978-0-231-16965-3 (pbk. : alk. paper)
ISBN 978-0-231-85057-5 (e-book)

Columbia University Press books are printed on permanent and durable acid-free paper.
This book is printed on paper with recycled content.

Printed in the United States of America

p 10 9 8 7 6 5 4 3 2 1

CONTENTS

Remembering F. B. Smith, T. B. Burtt, C. C. Burke, G. F. Cresswell, G. O. Rabone, H. B. Cave, J. A. Hayes, J. R. Reid, F. L. H. Mooney, B. Sutcliffe, V. J. Scott, W. M. Wallace, W. A. Hadlee, M. P. Donnelly, J. Cowie.

ACKNOWLEDGEMENTS

Thanks to old friends and colleagues Peter Evans, Ron Guariento and John Saunders for many insights over the years. Also to Noel Brown and Charles Barr who commented on early versions of the manuscript. To Ho-Kyung Kim for her help with Korean matters. To Michael Munro for preventing the loss of an early draft. To the New Zealand Film Archive for giving me access to a copy of *Old Scores*. To Yoram Allon at Wallflower Press for commissioning this book and then seeing it to publication. Finally, to my father from whom I inherited my love of sports and to my mother with whom I saw my first films.

INTRODUCTION:
START OF PLAY

A few introductory words about Invictus

Invictus (Clint Eastwood, 2010) is a useful point to begin a short account of
the sports film. A recent, high profile production, with two actors (Morgan
Freeman as Nelson Mandela and Matt Damon as François Pienaar, the captain of the South African rugby team) nominated for Academy Awards, and
a major contemporary American director in Eastwood, it attests both to the
contemporary prestige of the proliferating sports film, and to the interna-
tionalising of the genre. Films such as *Cry Freedom* (Richard Attenborough,
1987), *Cry the Beloved Country* (Darrell Roodt, 1995), *The Power of* One
(John G. Avildsen, 1992), *A Dry White Season* (Euzhan Palcy, 1989), and
Goodbye Bafana (Billie August, 2007), demonstrate the contemporary
cinema's fascination with the South African apartheid regime and its fall,
and with the figure of Nelson Mandela, widely seen as one of the political
heroes of our time. Another film about this era might have been expected,
but hardly a Hollywood production based on the 1995 Rugby World Cup,
rugby being a lower tier sport in the US (the largely forgotten progenitor of
American football), and Hollywood faithfully reflecting American parochial-
ism as regards other nations' sports.

Like many of the most memorable sports films, *Invictus* through its
sports narrative addresses not just sporting matters but wider issues,
not implicitly as many do, but very explicitly, thus providing an overt
opening example of the genre's workings. Its narrative centres on
Mandela's attempts as the new first President of post-apartheid South
Africa (1994) to create a moment of reconciliation and popular unity in
the newly designated 'Rainbow Nation' around the national team in the

1995 Rugby World Cup played in South Africa, an unlikely project because the 'Springbok' rugby team had throughout the century been a preeminent icon of Afrikaaner white supremacy. Given this, the segregated non-white sections of crowds at test matches against other rugby playing countries notoriously supported the opposition against the national team. Mandela, in pursuit of his seemingly impossible vision, enlists the unlikely support of François Pienaar, and through him, slowly, the backing of the overwhelmingly Afrikaaner team, with its one black player, Chester Watson. The desired change in attitude among the minority but economically powerful whites and the numerically dominant black population (football rather than rugby supporters) is microcosmically shown through the interactions of the President's security men, an unwilling mixture of ANC Africans and apartheid-era whites, and of the Pienaar household of the captain's conservative parents and their black maid. As this précis suggests, *Invictus* – and in this it is typical of the great majority of sports films – is an example of conservative, classical filmmaking, employing strategies (like the larger thematic being relayed through individuals and small groups) familiar to the viewer.

Like many sports films, *Invictus* also drives to a final encounter in which the South African team faces the all-conquering New Zealand All Blacks, with their seemingly unstoppable giant winger Jonah Lomu. The final is won narrowly by the Springboks, leading to national rejoicing, representatively individualised in the cameo of the black boy trying to listen to the initially hostile white policemen's radio broadcasting the game, and joyfully celebrating with them at its end. That many of the All Blacks were suffering from the effects of food poisoning that some have claimed was a deliberate act is not mentioned in the narrative, which might be more complex with it, but would certainly be less forceful and exemplary.

Released fifteen years after the events of 1995, as South Africa struggled with seemingly intractable socio-political, economic and racial problems, the film was in some quarters accused of suggesting naïvely that momentary feelings generated by a sporting victory had banished the nation's many troubles. That the film, like many sports films, is an inspirational story, drawing on the not wholly rational emotions aroused by national sporting success, is obvious, but it is intelligent enough to know that it is celebrating a symbolic moment of unity that may be hard to sustain and live up to, as indeed it has been. If one might point a moral for this book through the film and its reception, it is that sports films should be read with the same intelligence given to, indeed demanded for, other forms of popular generic cinema.

A very abbreviated history of the sports film

The moving photographic image and organised sport as recognised today, both developments of the late nineteenth century and dominating features of life since, have had a continuingly close relationship. Sports films, either 'actualities' or brief fictions, appear early in the American, British and French cinemas (and those of Australia and New Zealand, both profoundly sports orientated British colonial cultures), reflecting the late nineteenth century rise in spectator sports: e.g. *The Leonard–Cushing Fight* (Edison Kinetoscope, US, 1894), *The Oxford and Cambridge Boat Race* (Birt Acres and Robert W. Paul, UK, 1895), *The 1896 Derby* (Paul, UK, 1896), *The Melbourne Cup* (Australia, 1896), *Football* (Lumière Brothers, France, 1897), *The Ball Game* (Edison, US, 1898), *Auckland Cup* (NZ, 1898), *Races at Poona* (India, 1898), *Blackburn versus West Bromwich* (UK, 1898), *Dr. [W.G.] Grace's Jubilee Procession* (UK, 1989), *Casey at the Bat* (US, 1899), *Comic Boxing Match* (UK, 1900), *Boy's Cricket Match and Fight* (UK, 1900), *Leçon de Boxe* (Lumière Brothers, France, circa 1901–3), *Ping Pong* (UK, 1902), *The New Zealand Footballers: The All Blacks' Reception and Arrival at Auckland* (NZ, 1906), fragments of the England v South Africa cricket test at Newlands (South Africa, 1906), and, most extraordinarily, the ninety-minute-long Veriscope *Corbett–Fitzsimmons Fight* (Enoch J. Rector, US, 1897), now recognised as the first feature length film. (Some of these, with others, are listed in McKernan, 1996). New as they were, these early films are part of a historical continuum of visual representations, which includes many classical Greek examples of runners, throwers (e.g. Myron's 'Discobolus' statue which memorably comes to life at the beginning of Riefenstahl's *Olympia*), boxers, wrestlers, and horse racers, with the javelin throwing sequences by the 'Carpenter' and 'Colmar' painters, pre-motion picture capturing of action sequences, and nineteenth century British paintings, as well as literary records of sports from Pindar's fifth century BC Odes to winners at the various Panhellenic Games, to nineteenth century English writing (e.g. Hazlitt's essays 'The Fight' and 'The Indian Jugglers', and Thomas Hughes' *Tom Brown's Schooldays*).

3

Zucker and Babich's *Sports Films: A Complete Reference* (1987) lists around 2000 feature length and early short films. Since the 1960s, the genre's output has accelerated tremendously, until in the last few decades more sports-based features have been made, especially in the US, than ever before, underwriting the domination sport and the discourse of sport have over daily life, and the sports star's status as the time's most central 'hero of consumption' (Leo Lowenthal's oft-quoted phrase from his essay 'Biographies in Popular Magazines'). Clearly, no short book could cover such a large, constantly expanding genre. Thus this one, though wishing to demonstrate the genre's extensiveness and multifacetedness, attempts depth rather than impossible comprehensiveness, concentrating on a small proportion of the 170 or so films in its filmography (itself highly selective), chosen to demonstrate patterns and preoccupations, changes and developments across the genre.

Some preliminary definitions

Whether seen as a genre, or as a looser grouping with a 'special relation to narrative' (Gary Whannel 2008: 81) which can be attached to a multitude of genres and sub-genres, the sports film's longstanding contemporary boom reverses Hollywood's traditional views of its doubtful viability. Against the claim that sports films lack such generic attributes as a typical *mise-en-scène*, a characteristic style, and auteurs, there are various answers: that the typical *mise-en-scène* is the sports stadium or games playing site, the 'field of dreams', that a major part of the genre's iconography consists of the materials of and surrounding sport, and that to define a genre by whether or not highly regarded individual directors have made careers in it is eccentric. However, the list of distinguished film makers who have made sports films is a long one, running from Lindsay Anderson, Robert Aldrich and Anthony Asquith to Leni Riefenstahl, Robert Rossen, Martin Scorsese, Oliver Stone, Robert Towne and David Williamson, the Australian writer of *The Four Minute Mile* (Jim Goddard, 1988) and *The Club* (Bruce Beresford, 1980). The further claim that sports films lack 'a consistent set of themes, images or tropes' is demonstrably mistaken, with Whannel, the source of the arguments disagreed with above, himself contributing his master theme of gaining and losing 'respect' or 'acceptance' to the sports film's primary thematics. Additionally, it is doubtful that other genres exhibit more characteristic styles (outside of fixed periods) than the sports film. This book then treats the sports film as a genre, but claims that its analyses will still be found relevant if the reader disagrees. It also finds the sports film, for all its variety, the 'coherent category' Whannel denies, a curious position given that his insightful particular analyses characteristically imply its coherence rather than incoherence (Whannel 2008: 80–2).

Hollywood's historical predominance means that the sports film has been dominated not just by American films but by American films about American sports. Further, most writing on it is also American, underscoring the parochial assumptions that the sports film means both American sport and American film. By contrast, this book, while acknowledging Hollywood's centrality, locates the genre across the British (English, Scottish, Welsh), Indian, Australian, New Zealand, Canadian, Iranian, Japanese, South Korean, Thai, French, German, Danish and other cinemas. This (i) challenges the over-identification of the sports film with Hollywood; (ii) brings into view sports neglected in American films; (iii) dramatises the meanings of different sports in different cultures, and (iv) because non-Hollywood films belong to alternative cinematic traditions, expands our sense of the genre's possibilities.

This book employs a definition of sports as organised, physical, rule-bound contests between individuals or teams (or even against the self), so this excludes blood sports, although there are distinguished bullfighting films, and other contests of humans against animals, meaning the omission of another filmic subject, the rodeo. However, the popular cinematic topic of horseracing – which might be defined as animal/human collaboration, a kind of centaurism – is included. Some readers might wish to exclude the most atavistic of sports, boxing, but it is so central to the sports film that its omission is impossible. Also sidelined are games of total chance or purely intellectual skills; contests whose mock-agon is wholly theatrical, e.g. modern professional wrestling, despite its fan followings and admirers (Roland Barthes' 'The World of Wrestling' in *Mythologies*, and WWE's television audiences); bodybuilding, male and female, where, though *Pumping Iron II* (George Butler, 1985) is a favoured site for critics interested in deconstructing sex and gender norms, the kinds of contest and skills associated with sports as defined here are lacking; and finally grotesqueries like speed or bulk eating, even though Huizinga in *Homo Ludens* refers to classical Greek bulk drinking contests (Huizinga 1970: 73).

Sports films are here defined as narratives *substantially* built around sports, rather than making the glancing allusions to them common wherever they are an important part of a culture. Films where sport's role is substantial necessarily intersect with other genres and modes (comedy, melodrama, the biopic, and so on), as they develop dramatic narratives to appeal beyond specialist audiences, treating themes often latent in the topoi of modern sports. These include for example, the public hero and the feelings he or she inspires, his or her rise (and/or fall), conflicts between the disciplines required by sports and other desires or duties, societal prejudices that may impede the sportsperson, male bonding through sports, and in some contemporary films, the female equivalent as well as father/son, mother/son, father/daughter and mother/daughter relationships. Important others are gaining or losing respect and acceptance (Whannel's master thematic), the temptations of fame, sport as a site of corruption (a thematic much in the air at the time of writing with the imprisonment of Pakistani test cricketers for a spot betting conspiracy and the revelations of the cyclist Lance Armstrong's drug-taking), the prime and decline of the body, sport as an instrument of class, ethnic, sex, gender, regional or national identity and assertion, the tension between the individual and the group, and the meaning of various sports in nations' consciousness. And, in the contemporary era, sport as a central instance of the commodification of life, but also as a precious sphere of utopian feeling, of what David Foster Wallace (describing the tennis player Federer) calls 'kinetic beauty', an experience of being reconciled to the body, whether experienced or watched (Wallace 2006). Or as William Hazlitt wrote of the great fives player Kavanagh, in what might be an allegory of all modes of self-command and achievement, 'His eye was certain, his hand fatal, his presence of mind complete. He could do what he pleased, and he always knew completely what to do' (Hazlitt 1982: 131).

Because of sport's place in so many lives, its carrying so many meanings, both utopian and dystopian, many films that cannot be called sports films feature sequences where a sport is invoked in ways more developed than mere passing allusions. For instance, the sports moments in the exhilarating newsreel montage beginning the Australian film *Newsfront* (Philip Noyce, 1978) – harness racing, cricket, swimming, tennis, gymnastics – and the same film's climactic narrative use of the Hungary versus USSR water polo brawl (provoked by the Russian invasion of Hungary) at the 1956 Melbourne Olympics, have important meanings because of the centrality of sport in Australian life and memory, and sport's connections with politics and nationality worldwide. Also, with *Newsfront* being a meta -filmic movie about newsreel filmmakers, these moments testify to film's longstanding attraction to sport as the quintessence of 'moving pictures'. Likewise, a whole nexus of politics, cultural assertion, conflict, and mythology, is invoked in two recent historical films set in early twentieth century Ireland, *Michael Collins* (Neil Jordan, 1996), where British forces invade Croke Park, killing spectators, during a Limerick versus Dublin Gaelic Football game, and *The Wind That Shakes the Barley* (Ken Loach, 2006) where men playing recreational hurling are brutally arrested by the Black and Tans. In both films, Gaelic sports symbolise the conflict between Britain and Ireland, with the Gaelic Athletic Association banned by the British in 1918, and participation in or even watching British games banned by the GAA until as late as 1971. Clearly, neither of these films is a sports film, despite the importance of the scenes noted. However, they and others like the cricket match in *The Go-Between* (Joseph Losey, 1970), demonstrate how a single scene in a film not centrally about sport, can embody more intensely some of the meanings of a particular sport than films where the concern is pervasive but the meanings enacted unremarkable.

Where films are substantially built around sports, they obviously qualify as sports films, but the question is where to draw the line, how 'substantial' is 'substantial'? This is ultimately a problem of genre categorisation and not resolvable in any absolute way. Films centred throughout on sports performers and performances give rise to few ambiguities of categorisation but in other films the sports thematic, though present, may be less constant and less central. When does a film with war scenes become a war film? When does a film with songs become a musical? While there is no doubt about *Rocky*'s (John G. Avildsen, 1976) centrality to the genre, in Luchino Visconti's *Rocco and His Brothers/Rocco e i suoi Fratelli* (1960), where boxing plays an important symbolic role, we are likely to feel less that it is the generator of the film's extended meanings than a particular manifestation of them and that for this reason the film belongs on the most distant fringes of the genre, a film in which the sport has an important role, but hardly a sports film. *Gregory's Girl* (Bill Forsyth, 1981) stays in the memory as a football film through its early parts – in particular Dorothy's breaking into the boys' football team and the lovestruck

Sporting girls, modern inflection, in *Bend It Like Beckham*

Gregory's inept goalkeeping as he helps her to practice. But it moves away from football into a rites of passage narrative where Gregory is redirected by the girls towards a more feasible relationship, with football playing no further part. Yet the football sequences are so memorable, so integral to the film's delineations of character, masculinity and femininity, that though, like *Rocco*, it hardly qualifies as a sports film, it has a place on the genre's borders. This is in contrast to the centrality of the game in another British football film, *Bend It Like Beckham* (Gurinder Chadha, 2003) where Jesminder, the British Sikh heroine's trajectory is constantly linked to her passion for the game, and through it to the film's larger statements about female assertion and British Indian diaspora thematics. Lindsay Anderson, answering the difficult question what his film *This Sporting Life* (1963), set in the northern English world of rugby league, is 'about', argues that it 'is not a film about sport', but rather a film 'about a man ... of extraordinary power and aggressiveness, both temperamental and physical, but at the same time with a great innate sensitiveness and need for love of which he is at first hardly aware'. The 'world of Rugby League football' is the 'particular social setting of the film', its 'significant background ... of the kind of people who make up the game, the exploiters and the exploited and the spectators who live vicariously off them...' (Anderson 2004: 92–3). In that the film gives no sense of how the City team progresses, and next to none of the game's tactics other than its toughness, the director's statement is understandable, but the significance of the game and its institutional structures are such that it is hard to imagine the film without them (the game's hardness, its importance to a down at heel Northern English city, its escape route from mining, its lack of glamour and so on). Football with its greater glamour and economic rewards, would not be the same, while the individualist sport of boxing could not intersect with the team elements of the game and the team's place in the city's life.

This book is a brief *poetics* or *anatomy* of a genre. The sports film has recently often been discussed as a regressive site of white masculinism, and racial, sex, gender and class oppression. Clearly such accusations raise important issues, but for this book the complex meanings of sports and sports films are not wholly reducible to such questions. They must be included because sport, while paradoxically a boundaried world of arbitrary self-enclosed convention and liberating meaninglessness, is also always closely bound to social meaning, where, as C.L.R. James in *Beyond a Boundary* wrote of his West Indian cricketing youth, 'selected individuals played representative roles which were charged with social significance' (James 1963: 72). James also took issue with Bernard Berenson in claiming that sports embodied 'significant [aesthetic] form' (see James 1963: 191–206), thus acknowledging both realities. A *poetics* of the genre should cover all important aspects of its films, including their narrative forms, their cross–generic interrelations, their formal conventions, their specific investment in spectacle, the histories of particular sports and cinemas, the interconnection of sport, cinema and nation, the positive and negative mythologies they embody, the circle comprising sport, cinema and social context, tradition and change. It should also address – which the most ideologically oriented criticism seldom does – the affirmative pleasures that sport and by extension artistic representations of sport give even in the consumerist and regimen driven world of contemporary sport to both participants and audiences. In the English poet Edmund Blunden's book *Cricket Country* (published in 1944 when major organised sport in Britain was suspended and therefore viewed very nostalgically), he claims that 'Somewhere I read the last letter of a man who was about to be hanged for a murder, and as I remember it, it bore a postscript, "No more cricket, George"' (Blunden 1944: 18). Just as the trope embodied in the baseball film *Field of Dreams* (Phil Alden Robinson, 1989) of the protagonist building a field on which the ghosts of players past can play again, might appeal to the followers of any other sport, so too might Blunden's condemned lover of one particular sport appeal to that of any other, who would recognise the sentiment involved.

The sports film and genre

'Yes, I have taken my stab at the wrestlin' form.'
– Bill Mayhew in *Barton Fink* (Coen Brothers, 1991)

Although sports fictions have always been prolific in the American cinema, references to a sports genre were rare until recently, though boxing, football, baseball and horse and motor racing films were frequently noted as distinct types in the 1930s (see Neale 2000: 233–36). Arguably the distinctiveness of these dominant sub-types, recently joined by the prolific contemporary American basketball film, each with its own history, ethos and spectacle, discouraged the deeper categorising which registers underlying similarities rather than surface differences. Though the British cinema produced early sports films, its output, as overall, has been much smaller. Marcia Landy's study of British genres between 1930 and 1960 includes only a few films based on sports, always placed in overriding categories like tragic melodrama (Landy 1991). More recently Charles Barr's *Encyclopedia of British Cinema* 'Sports Films' entry (Barr 2003: 630–31) implied a genre's existence and made comparisons with American sports films, an example followed by Glen Jones (2005). The moral here is that perception of a phenomenon depends a great deal on the observer's attitude; i.e. some commitments secondarise signs of the sports genre, while an interest in sport asserts them. The small number of sports-based fiction films in the Russian, German, French and Spanish and other European cinemas, obviously discouraged generic classification (though these histories are areas too specialised to be explored here), though now the sports film tends to be described as a genre, one can see tendencies towards generic recognition worldwide.

In the last two decades the category 'sports film' has become naturalised and uncontentious, as surfing the internet demonstrates. 'IMDb's Top Fifty Sports Movies', 'ESPN.com Top Twenty Sports Movies of All Time', '*Sports Illustrated*'s Top 50 Sports Movies', 'The Most Overused Sports

Movie Clichés', 'The Ten Greatest Sports Movie Motivational Speeches', the latter two, beneath their banality, appealing to audience knowledge of conventions shared by many sub-types (in the clichés list 'A down and out coach is given one last shot ... the players overcome race relations or gang violence, and are brought together by being a team... The coach can't get along with his star player' – all moments applicable to many sports and, for all the list's Americanness, to many places of origin). The recent accelerated production of sports-based films, the variety of sports treated in these mitigating the dominance of the major kinds and suggesting the need for a more capacious category, the increasing prominence of 'foreign' sports films – eg. *Chariots of Fire*'s (Hugh Hudson, 1981) Academy Awards (1982), *Lagaan*'s (Ashutosh Gowariker, 2002) best foreign film Academy Award nomination (2002), the international success of *Bend It Like Beckham* – advancing recognition of a film type made internationally, can all be seen as contributing to recognition of a sports genre.

Sports fiction films largely follow the pattern described by Bordwell, Thompson and Staiger in *The Classical Hollywood Cinema* film, 'causality, consequence, psychological motivations, the drive towards overcoming obstacles and achieving goals' (Bordwell et al. 1985: 13), the last at the heart of the American sports film, embodied in the repeated agon of the play off, final, championship decider, of so many plotlines. Existing in Hollywood's shadow, many non-American sports films echo this, also following another highly overt pattern defined in *The Classical Hollywood Cinema* where a second line of action intersects the first with heterosexual romantic love (Bordwell et al. 1985: 16–17), whether happy (*Rocky*), tragic (*The Hustler,* Robert Rossen, 1961), or marginal (*The Miracle of Bern/Das Wunder von Bern,* Sönke Wortmann, 2003), with occasional latent, seldom open, homosexual variants (*Personal Best,* Robert Towne, 1982; *L'Air de Paris*, Marcel Carné, 1954).

Romantic plots are particularly foregrounded in the paradigm of generic hybridity arising from the conjoining of the sports genre with romantic comedy. Films like *Pat and Mike* (George Cukor, 1952), *Bull Durham* (Ron Shelton, 1998), *Tin Cup* (Ron Shelton, 1996) and *Fever Pitch* (David Evans, 1997) work the conventions of romantic comedy, but are played out by couples characteristic of the romantic comedy/sports hybrid: male athlete or fan paired with female non-athlete or non-fan (*Tin Cup, Fever Pitch, Leatherheads*, George Clooney, 2008), male athlete with female manager

The sports film/
romantic comedy
hybrid in *Pat and Mike*

(*The Main Event*, Howard Zieff, 1979), female athlete with male manager (*Pat and Mike*, George Cukor, 1952), male athlete with female fan (*Bull Durham*), male athlete with female athlete (*Wimbledon*, Richard Loncraine, 2004). One of the reasons the sports film and romantic comedy combine so successfully is the fact that sport is such a complex shifting area of attitudes to masculinity and femininity, questions often vexed and hostility provoking, but given pleasurable exercise in romantic comedy's male/female interactions.

Being a genre of considerable plasticity, defined by an action based around sport, the sports film is particularly open to hybridity as the sports narrative attaches itself to different modes and sub-generic categories. A list using only films in the filmography might include at least the following, while noting that particular films often require multiple categories:

– romantic comedy – *Pat and Mike, Bull Durham, Tin Cup*
– the biopic – *The Joe Louis Story* (Robert Gordon, 1953), *Pride of the Yankees* (Sam Wood, 1942), *Dawn!* (Ken Hannam, 1979)
– silent comedy – *The Freshman* (Harold Lloyd, 1925), *College* (James W. Horne, 1927), *Pool Sharks* (Edwin Middleton, 1915)
– broad comedy – *Caddyshack* (Harol Ramis, 1988), *Mike Bassett England Manager* (Steve Barron, 2001), *Iron Ladies/Satri Lek* (Yongyuth Thongonthung, 2000)
– sophisticated comedy – *The Final Test* (Anthony Asquith, 1953), *The Main*

Event, Old Scores (Alan Clayton, 1991)
- the fan film – *Fever Pitch* (David Evans, 1997), *Looking for Eric* (Ken Loach, 2009) *Field of Dreams*
- documentary – *Olympia* (Leni Riefenstahl, 1938), *Hoop* Dreams (Steve James, 1994), *When We Were Kings* (Leon Gast and Taylor Hackford, 1996)
- the history film – *8 Men Out* (John Sayles, 1988), *The Four Minute Mile*, *The Damned United* (Tom Hooper, 2009)
- the feminist film – *Chak De India!* (Shimit Amin, 2007), *Bend it Like Beckham*, *Heart Like a Wheel* (Jonathan Kaplan, 1983)
- the musical – *Take Me out to the Ball Game* (Busby Berkeley, 1949), *Damn Yankees* (George Abbott and Stanley Donen, 1958)
- the family film – *National Velvet* (Michael Curtiz, 1944), *The Bad News Bears* (Michael Ritchie, 1976)
- fantasy – *Field of Dreams*, *Damn Yankees*, *Angels in the Outfield* (Clarence Brown, 1951)
- the art film – *The Goalkeeper's Fear of the Penalty/Die Angst der Tormanns beim Elfmeter* (Wim Wenders, 1972)
- the social problem exposé film – *The Harder They Fall* (Mark Robson, 1956), *Requiem for a Heavyweight* (Ralph Nelson, 1962)
- the teenage rites of passage film – *Breaking Away* (Peter Yates, 1980), *Australian Rules* (Paul Goldman, 2002), (*Blue Crush* (John Stockwell, 2003)
- the race film – *The Jackie Robinson Story* (Alfred E. Green, 1950), *Australian Rules*, *Playing Away* (Horace Ové, 1987)
- the cross-cultural film – *Mister Baseball* (Fred Schepisi, 1992), *Lagaan* (Ashutosh Gowariker, 2002)
- the dystopic future film – *Rollerball* (Norman Jewison, 1975), *Death Race 2000* (Paul Bartel, 1975)
- psychological melodrama – *The Hustler*, *Fear Strikes Out* (Robert Mulligan, 1957), *Body and Soul* (Robert Rossen, 1947)
- the thriller – *The Fan* (Tony Scott, 1996)
- the detective film – *The Arsenal Stadium Mystery* (Thorold Dickinson, 1939)
- the road movie – *Two Lane Black Top* (Monte Hellman, 1971), *Death Race 2000*
- the disabled athlete film – *Murderball* (Henry Alex Rubin and Dana Adam

Shapiro, 2005), *Ice Castles* (Donald Wrye, 2010), *Fear Strikes Out*
 – the genre parody film – *Movie Movie* (Stanley Donen, 1978), *Sports Movie* (David Koechner, 2007)
 – the gay or transsexual affirmation film – *Iron Ladies, Beautiful Boxer* (Ekachai Eukrongtham, 2003)
 – the 1940s/50s Woman's film – *Hard, Fast and Beautiful* (Ida Lupino, 1951)
 – the horror film – *I Know How Many Runs You Scored Last Summer* (Stacey Edmonds and Doug Turner, 2008), *Tzameti 13* (Géla Babluani, 2005)

Generic hybridity extends beyond interaction with a single genre. *Bend It Like Beckham*, for example, is hardly unusual in its multiple affiliations: with the feminist film, as female marginality in male-dominated sports is challenged by Jesminder's footballing ambitions; with the cross-cultural film, where the heroine as a diasporic London Punjabi Sikh is caught between two cultures; with the teenage rites of passage film; with the buddy film (female version, Jesminder's and Julietta's friendship), and, more broadly, with comedy. Additionally, each sport that becomes a repeated film subject constitutes a micro-genre, with its own variations on the genre's iconography and *mise-en-scène* – the athletics film, the golf film, the baseball film, the surfing film, the cricket film, the rugby (union or league) film, the motor racing film, the karate or kung fu film (*The Karate Kid*, 1984 and 2010), the basketball film, the ice hockey film, the tennis film, the cycling film, the skating film, the football (soccer) film, the American football film, the pool film, the lawn bowls film (*Crackerjack*, Paul Maloney, 2002, *Blackball*, Mel Smith, 2003), and so on.

To take an example of a sport restricted to one cinema, the Australian Rules football film (of which there are only three major fictional examples, *The Great MacArthy*, David Baker, 1975, *The Club*, Bruce Beresford, 1980, and *Australian Rules*, Paul Goodman, 2002, as well as various documentaries). Though sharing with other sports films a broadly similar 'semantic field' and 'syntactic' (structural) tendencies, it has a specific *mise-en-scène* and iconography, its big oval playing areas, its rules and plays, the goal umpires dressed like cricket umpires, the spectacular mark, the dress spectacle of the players' sleeveless singlets, revealing with the typically brief shorts, more of the male body than most sports. It is also a game where there is marked ethnic and aboriginal participation, so that one of the films, *Australian Rules*, is not only a teenage rites of passage film but a race film (distinguished from the cross-cultural film by the presence of serious racial prejudice). Further, played little internationally, it presents itself as quintessentially Australian. Another example, the horse racing film, historically and internationally prolific, is, alongside boxing and pool films, the most likely to involve criminality, e.g. bribing of jockeys (*The Rainbow Jacket* (Basil Dearden, 1954) and doping or killing of horses (*Phar Lap*, Simon Wincer, 1983).

Whether American, British or Australian, horse racing narratives often tend to social panorama – aristocracy, or virtual aristocracy, moneyed middle class owners, the usually more lower end jockeys and so on, particularly clear both in the Australian *Phar Lap* and the British *The Rainbow Jacket*, with, in the more egalitarian Australian instance, the high society rulers of racing unappealingly presented, rather like the millionaire owner of War Admiral, Seabiscuit's rival in *Seabiscuit* (Gary Ross, 2003). In *Phar Lap* and *Seabiscuit* the animal protagonist becomes a national symbol, also providing the link for the human relationships that take place around him. This sub-type, like others, has its own distinctive *mise-en-scène* and iconography – legal and illegal betting sites, the jockeys' weighing in, idyllic training sequences, the pre-race parade, the (*après* Dégas and Dufy) spectacle of the jockeys' silks, the race horses at full stretch (whether in flat racing, steeplechasing, e.g. the biopic *Champions*, John Irvin, 1984, or harness racing/trotting e.g. *Green Grass of Wyoming*, Louis King, 1948). As a particularly prolific sub-type, it exhibits many cross-generic forms, visible in various racing comedies (e.g. the Marx Brothers' *A Day at the Races*, Sam Wood, 1937) or pastoral dramas (e.g. *Green Grass of Wyoming*), different in tone from urban instances. A less obvious example, *National Velvet*, is both an example of the family film and, with its young heroine encouraged by her ex-Channel swimming mother, an early, rather fantastical instance of the feminist sports film. Readers might, following the above, here sketch the properties of other sub-types that interest them, e.g. the surfing film, the ice hockey film, the tennis film, the golf film, and so on.

Plots and superplots

In the Coen Brothers' *Barton Fink* an earnest New York (Clifford Odets-like) socially-conscious dramatist struggles in Hollywood to write at a (Louis B.Mayer-like) executive's behest, a wrestling film. 'Wally Beery is a wrestler, I want to know his hopes, his dreams. Naturally he'll have to get mixed up with a bad element. And a romantic interest, you know the drill. Or else a young kid, an orphan. Which is it...? Orphan? Dame? Both maybe? ... What do you want – a roadmap?' The comic monologue exposes the sports film through one of its less elevated instances, as banally predictable.

Such predictability is burlesqued in *Sports Movie* (David Koechner, 2007) which travesties such fixtures as the failing coach facing his last chance, the danger to his marriage of his sporting obsessions, the hopeless team magically metamorphosed into irresistible winners, and sport's homoerotic as well as heteroerotic potentialities, along with fleeting sendups of *Bend It Like Beckham and Field of Dreams*. Donen's *Movie Movie* parody/burlesques a 'Warren Brothers' 1930s boxing film. This, 'Dynamite Hands', features an ethnic New York background (*cf. Golden Boy*, Rouben Mamoulian, 1939, *Body and Soul*, Robert Rossen, 1947), a Jewish hero Joey Popchik (*Body and Soul*), his Irish librarian girlfriend, Betsy McGuire, tenement rooftop scenes (*Golden Boy, Body and Soul*) with Betsy caring for her pigeons parodying Brando's ex-boxer with Eve Marie Saint in *On the Waterfront (Elia Kazan, 1954)*. Exaggerated stereotypes include the tough but honest manager, the smooth gangster–fixer and the expensive showgirl who seduces the fighter (Grace in *Champion*, Mark Robson, 1949, Alice in *Body and Soul*), the hero torn between fighting to fund his sister's eye operation and studying law (*Golden Boy*'s struggle between fighting and the violin), and oft-repeated situations: the hero's punching power accidentally discovered (*Golden Boy, The Milky Way*, Harold Lloyd, 1936), the gangster proposing a dive ('I guess you didn't see tomorrow's papers. You were knocked out in the fifth round', *The Set-Up* (Robert Wise, 1949), *Raging Bull* (Martin Scorsese, 1980), *Body and Soul,* the protagonist, though agreeing to lose, unable to resist knocking out his opponent. These burlesqued conventions are specific to the boxing sub-genre, but have parallels over the whole field, as *Sports Movie* demonstrates.

Such generic predictability is often undeniable. The basic plot of many, even most, sports films is the overcoming of odds by individual or team, culminating in a final contest in which a last minute victory is gained. This is equally as true of distinguished as undistinguished films, and is the reason why sports have been described as having 'a special relation to narrative'. 'A sport event poses the question, "who will win?", and promises an answer to that question', the question and its usually affirmative answer having intimate relations to the 'Celebration of winning, of success, of achievement and of fame [which] occupies a significant place in western cultures' (most obviously the USA) (Whannel 2008: 81, 85), though communist countries such as the former DDR, Soviet Russia and China have equally, if not more fanatically, sought victory in sport for ideological ends. A frequent accompanying central action, in team sports narratives, follows the building of the team from antagonistic individuals into a unit, a plot active in other genres where the group is paramount – e.g. the war film or the backstage musical. The group's divisions may be racial, as in *Remember the Titans* (Boaz Yakin, 2000) where the black and white members of the High School football team as well as the black coach and deposed white coach have to cooperate to succeed, of ethnicity, or class, of insiders and outsiders, or caused by narcissistic stars. The women's hockey film *Chak De India!* (Shimit Amin, 2007) is an excellent example, with its coach, a Muslim outsider, having to create unity (transparently equated with Indian national homogeneity) out of many conflicting psychological types with differing regional loyalties, and overcome class conflicts as well as narcissistic star tendencies. In the Thai volleyball film *Iron Ladies* coach Bee has to deal with her *katoeis*' (ladyboys) flamboyant differences, sexual squabbles and emotional vicissitudes, melding them into national champions.

Variations on the victory plot

The victory plot, apparently so simple, is capable of many different inflections and in this it is comparable to the equally predictable, equally differentiated final unions of romantic comedy. Consider these complicating instances. (i) There may be two endings, the first pessimistic, the second optimistic, turning the first either into a momentary pessimistic misperception, or leaving it as the more likely closure, depending on the viewer's input. Near the end of the surfing film *Big Wednesday* (John Milius, 1978), when Matt turns up at the pier the night before the big swell, and talks to the surfing guru 'Bear' of his old companions arriving in the morning, 'Bear' dismisses this as fantasy, yet, come the morning, the trio are reunited. (ii) The final victory may be (intentionally) formulaic, to the extent that its conventional upbeat pleasures hardly outweigh the narrative's subversions. For instance, that ebulliently satirical comedy *The Club* (1980) climaxes with the failing Collingwood team, racked by on- and off-field feuds, winning the final to an upbeat Australian Rules anthem. Yet the film's main body is so subversive of inspirational cliché, that it is difficult for any sophisticated viewing to forget such dominant effects. (iii) Triumph is shadowed by loss. In *The Hustler* (Robert Rossen, 1961) 'Fast Eddie' eventually triumphs over Minnesota Fats, but his break up with his gambler patron means that he will never play again, and the suicide of Sarah, a victim of his ambition, renders the victory dreadfully compromised. At the close of *Downhill Racer* (Michael Ritchie, 1969) David Chappelet's skiing triumph appears vulnerable in his fleeting encounter with the rising star who may displace him. *Gentleman Jim* (Raoul Walsh, 1942), the biopic of the heavyweight champion James J. Corbett, seems unsullied in its romantic and rambunctious resolutions, but nevertheless remains haunted by the defeated champion, John L. Sullivan's, appearance at Corbett's victory party, bringing with him intimations of the inevitability of decline and defeat for everyone, including the momentarily touched and melancholy Corbett. (iv) Winning while losing. In *Cool Runnings* (John Turteltaub, 1993), the Jamaican bobsledders achieve their quixotic dream of making the Winter Olympics although none of them (except their coach) has ever seen snow, put in a good time, but crash out because of inferior equipment. Nevertheless their hope and courage win over the crowd and an end title relates that they competed in the next winter Olympics 'as equals'. Here victory is redefined as taking part, a return to the ethos of De Coubertin, the founder of the modern Olympics, gaining the pride of being an Olympian, good enough to compete at the top. One of the best known sports films, *Rocky*, follows a not-dissimilar pattern, with the prelim fighter, pulled out of obscurity for promotional purposes, losing to the world champion, Apollo Creed – since a lower tier fighter winning would stretch credulity too much – but, in so nearly achieving an upset, attaining glory. After the uncomplicated wishfulfilment victory plots of the following films of the *Rocky* franchise, *Rocky Balboa* (Sylvester Stallone, 2007) where the aged ex-champion comes out of retirement to take on the new titleholder, follows the same pattern of a loss so glorious it amounts to victory. In *Follow the Sun* (Sidney Lanfield, 1951), coming back after terrible injuries, just playing well in the tournament that ends the film is triumph enough for Ben Hogan. (v) Dual Concentrations: winners and others. In Fumihiko Suri's Japanese film *Ping Pong* (2002), there are dual protagonists, followed in their fortunes from childhood to secondary school table tennis stars. Here the juxtaposition is not simply victory against failure, but contrasts Peco's fulfilment of his driven wish to play in the German league with the more talented Smile's lesser commitment, seen not as failure, but the product of a less driven temperament, a choice with which he is happy. (vi) The Draw or Tie (Two Winners not One). In the charming New Zealand rugby comedy, *Old Scores* (Alan Clayton, 1991), because of the revelation that an international between Wales and New Zealand twenty years earlier was won by Wales through a touch judge's deliberately partial decision, the two rugby unions agree to replay the game but with the same now middle-aged players. In this instance of a narrative which rejects the more common partisanship of identifying with one team, for equal identification with both and the larger cultures they represent, the game is drawn, with honours even, when the ball kicked for the conversion that could win New Zealand the game rests on the crossbar, refusing to cross it.

Variations on the losing plot

But, generally, winners imply losers. A second overriding plot form, or group of plot forms, pursues an opposite trajectory, the relative rarity of which is explained by Ronald Bergan's noting how few American films dispense with winning plots, except temporarily where defeats along the way build character and eventual success, with only a few dramatising what John Huston, talking of his *Fat City* (1972), calls 'the spiritual processes of the defeated' (Bergan 1982: 7). In its simplest form this second plot negatively mirrors the victory plot with a final agon in which the protagonist(s) lose(s) rather than win(s). In the boxing films *Champion* (Mark Robson, 1949) and *The Square Ring* (Basil Dearden, 1953) the loss is literally of life, since the fighter dies after fighting – even though in both cases he has won, and the Mickey Rourke character is, it would seem, killed by his final bout in *The Wrestler* (Darren Aronofsky, 2008). In a different plot ordering, allowing for greater emphasis on those 'spiritual processes of the defeated', in *Requiem for a Heavyweight* (Ralph Nelson, 1962) the bout with the young Cassius Clay, as he then was, that ends Mountain Rivera's career, comes at the film's beginning, leading to his decline into the ignominy of professional wrestling. It is no accident that most of these examples are boxing films, since that sub-type is pre-eminently licensed to subvert the genre's usual optimism.

A film that is not exactly a sports film, but hovers at its edges, paralleling some of this second master plot's motifs, is *The Swimmer* (Frank Perry, 1968), from John Cheever's story, in which the ageing but still formidably athletic Burt Lancaster (Jim Thorpe in *Jim Thorpe All American*, Michael Curtiz, 1951), pursues an obscure quest to swim across the county's neighbouring suburban pools back to his home, while revelations about his ruined life emerge through encounters, until finally he finds his house locked up and desolate. As Lancaster journeys, wearing only swimming trunks, he fantasises about sports, injures his foot hurdling a barrier, and shivers in the autumnal wind. Though not exactly a sports film, *The Swimmer* might be seen as a kind of paradigm of its pessimistic tendencies. On the other hand, the losing plot has a more optimistic version where the ageing protagonist walks away, adjusted to the end of his career, on what are relatively his own terms in films as different as *North Dallas Forty* (Ted Kotcheff, 1979) and *The Final Test* (Anthony Asquith, 1953). Even celebratory biopics, if covering the sportsman's whole career, must include decline, as in *The Babe Ruth Story* (Roy Del Ruth, 1948) or *The Joe Louis Story*. A variation on losing the final agon, comes in *The Bad News Bears* (Michael Ritchie, 1976), where the children's coach (Walter Matthau), having driven them to the final by having the few best players monopolise team performances, has a moral epiphany, at the last moment letting the marginalised players participate, precipitating a defeat presented as more worthwhile than the win that could have been gained. In *Tin Cup* the golfing hero, with the US Open within his grasp, loses because he will not play safe, but is true to himself in attempting unsuccessfully the perfect shot he feels he should play. If in the former case winning is less important than the coach's moral choice, here winning is less important than truth to self.

A third elastic category

Such complex instances, troubling the simple win/lose schema so that it is sometimes unclear whether they should be considered complications of the victory or of the defeat plot, push towards a third, elastic category of less easily predictable plot forms characterised by their evasion of the winner/loser binarism or, if employing it, rendering it so faintly that it diminishes to a non-dominating point. For example, in Marcel Carné's

Surfing spectacle in *Big Wednesday*

L'Air de Paris, set in the boxing world, we never know whether the young boxer ever becomes a champion, since the narrative ends with him still a novice, and is primarily interested in the various relationships involving himself, his girlfriend, his trainer and the trainer's wife, with interesting emphasis placed on the homosocial/subterraneanly erotic plot between the trainer and boxer. *Big Wednesday* is a fine example of a narrative which evades the usual categorisations, at least in part because its central characters' surfing has (unlike that in the teen girl surfing film *Blue Crush*, John Stockwell, 2002) no formalised competition, with recognition of achievement coming from the informal judgement of one's peers, an unwritten tradition, recognised, however, in the surfing documentary *Liquid Dreams* shown late in the narrative which acknowledges Matt Johnson's and the others' predominance. Because surfing is in Pierre Bourdieu's terms a 'Californian' 'counter-cultural' youth sport (Giulianotti 2005: 164), in its pure form offering no financial rewards, no professional career, it is dependent on a protracted, protected middle class adolescent lifestyle eventually vulnerable to adulthood's pressures, most sinisterly here the Vietnam draft ('It seems like such a short time to be kids' as Mrs Barlow says, reminiscing years after with Matt). Hence of all sports films it is probably the most pervasively elegaic, the recognition of impermanence dominant even from its beginning where early on the surfing guru 'Bear' utters the warning 'nobody surfs for ever' and the film's very first words, spoken by its memorialising voiceover, are 'In the old days I remember a wind that would blow down the canyons...', setting the tone of its twelve year structure marked by seasons and swells and the characters' ageing.

The ambiguity of its double ending has already been noted, and even in its positive form it is marked by loss and elegy.

Sport and the art film

It is argued in chapter 3 that certain sports documentary sequences move towards the condition of the art film when the 'poetry of (sporting) motion' is emphasised over the sub-genre's usual priorities. Such moments in fiction films tend to be fleeting, momentary escapes from the demands of narrative cause and effect characteristic of formally conservative sports fictions as they embody that sense of sports as limited art forms, most memorably argued by C.L.R. James in *Beyond a Boundary* (James 1963: 191–206). This tendency to visual 'poetry' is only one possible aspect of the art film, a mode usually defined as foregrounding loosenings of narrative cause and effect, elliptical narration, ambiguous motivations, outcomes and symbolism, and blurring of the borders between objective realism and subjective interpretation. Unsurprisingly, given mainstream films' and audiences' resistance to such elements except as modified through their softened integration into mainstream post classical style (e.g. the filtering of elements of Soviet montage through MTV stylistics in *Any Given Sunday*, Oliver Stone, 1999, addressed in Chapter 4), the 'art film' entry above includes only one fiction film, Wim Wenders' *The Goalkeeper's Fear of the Penalty*. Even *The Swimmer,* at the genre's edges, is, except for its reticence as to the protagonist's motivations and immediate back story, classically structured. The two famous British films *The Loneliness of the Long Distance Runner* (Tony Richardson, 1962) and *This Sporting Life* depart from the dominant conventions of the sports film, with Frank (Richard Harris) drifting away from rugby league in the latter and Col (Tom Courtenay) in the former refusing to win the cross country race against the public school for the borstal governor. Both films are notable for their employment of expressive realism and that treatment of working class life which constituted an early 1960s rejuvenation of British film, but basically work within the conventions of the realist film, refreshing rather than subverting.

The Goalkeeper's Fear of the Penalty's protagonist, Bloch, a professional football goalkeeper, is first seen, inexplicably making no attempt to prevent a goal, then jostling the referee as he protests that the scorer was offside, kicking the ball away and being sent off. The narrative follows him over several days as he stays in small hotels, visits bars, plays jukeboxes, reads newspapers for the football scores, picks up girls, travels on trams or buses, twice gets into fights, visits an old girlfriend near the Yugoslav border, and early on, in an unpremeditated, unexplained *acte gratuit*, strangles a girl he has spent the night with, which lends a degree of mild suspense to his later peripatetic movements, reading of newspapers and occasional encounters with police or border guards, like the customs man who explains to him his technique for watching the way a suspect distributes his weight in order to guess in which direction he will attempt to escape. The film's last scene echoes this as Bloch, watching a local football game where a penalty is awarded, instructs a fellow spectator about the complex guessing game taking place between goalkeeper and penalty taker, with each knowing the other's most likely move, but having to guess whether he will vary it. Here the goalkeeper's calculation proves correct and he saves the goal, with the narrative drifting to an unresolved conclusion as the game continues. Heavily inscribed with Wenders' master theme of alienation, *The Goalkeeper's Fear of the Penalty* is not centrally about football, but uses elements of it as a metaphor or allegory, with the highly patterned rule-bound activity of the game contrasted with the arbitrariness of things beyond the pitch, and the referee's authority with the dubiety of social, psychological and moral meanings outside of the game.

1   DOMINANT PRESENCES: ONE

The sports biopic

The classical period biopic is the most conventional of Hollywood genres. For all its range of subjects, formulaic elements impose repetitive meanings on their apparent variety. As if to refute this, like other life-story films, sports biopics claim intimate factual authenticity for their inspirational accounts. Thus, *Knute Rockne All American* (1940) announces that its life of the Notre Dame football coach is 'based upon the private papers of Mrs Rockne and reports of Rockne's intimate anecdotes and friends'. Such 'facticity' typically privileges personal testimonies over more objective sources. Certainly sports biopics often display that detailed research with which studio Hollywood flourished its historical credentials, even as it shaped biographies into ideal forms disregarding ambiguities and opacities. In *Jim Thorpe All American* (1951), a Pennsylvania newspaper reporting Thorpe's college track feats surprisingly contains cricket reports, an arcanely authentic reminiscence of Philadelphia's forgotten cricketing past. Yet two of Thorpe's three wives and seven of his eight children disappear in the cause of dramatic symmetry, and the ageing athlete's inspirational conversion to coaching children and the framing banquet in his honour occlude his real life's poverty-stricken last years. His 1912 Olympics triumphs, loss of his gold medals and amateur status for playing baseball for subsistence money and 'Pop' Warner, his football coach and mentor, are factual, but sit alongside many inventions. As Robert Rosenstone says in the context of arguing the inevitability of contraction, displacement and condensation in all historical films, there is no absolute rule governing the legitimacy or otherwise of invention in fact-based narratives, but 'all such judgements must be decided on a case-by-case basis' (Rosenstone 2006: 46). Certainly Thorpe having only a single wife and child makes for a clearer, if more simplistic, narrative and the other changes have a rationale in the inspirational demands on biopics of the time. Georg Lukács justified historical novelists' and dramatists' (Shakespeare, Scott, Goethe, Schiller) inventions as transcending the 'pseudo historicism of the mere authenticity of individual facts', *if* the 'real historical validity' of such changes delineated underlying 'world historical' forces more cogently (Lukács 1969: 194–98), but the question arises with the classical biopic as to what are the forces of history and what merely of ideology masquerading as history? Its producer, Darryl F. Zanuck, defending inaccuracies in *Follow the Sun* (Sidney Lanfield, 1951), the Ben Hogan golfing biopic, claimed 'No one, in my opinion will ever pin us down to dates except the later dates in the past two or three years which are clearly remembered' (Custen 1992: 37–8), paralleled onscreen in *Jolson Sings Again* (Henry Levin, 1949) when the singer addresses his biopic's screenwriters: 'Let's agree about one thing at the start, boys. I don't think anybody cares about the facts of my life... What matters is the singing a man did and the difference that made'. The sports biopic replaces singing with hitting, running, and kicking, but retains overriding narrative conventions, including inevitable romance and marriage plots, and an eschewing of technicalities that might alienate uncommitted audiences. Thus, where Rockne's coaching innovations are sketched, the development of the forward pass is briefly explained, but the colourful myth of his deriving plays from chorus girls' precision dancing is more typical. Everywhere indeterminate histories are redrawn with uplifting moral clarity verging on hagiography, as in *The Babe Ruth Story* (1948). While Gehrig's untimely death in *The Pride of the Yankees* (Sam Wood, 1942) is haloed by religious auras, Ruth's is even more extreme, as he shortens what life remains by experimenting with an untried cancer treatment for the good of others. He also twice commits secular miracles as a crippled boy walks in response to a home run, and then one at death's door is revived by another.

Nevertheless, much as these sporting lives mirror other classical biopics' idealising, they also develop specific meanings ascribed to sport:

(i) American sports as a symbol of Americanness, with success in them a means of moving from society's margins to its centre; (ii) Sport, especially baseball, as an industrialised society's postlapsarian pastoral, though, paradoxically, as the product of industrialism, itself growingly industrialised, something generally obscured by the films; (iii) Sport as a site where tensions between the individual and the group, and between the drive for success and more restraining attitudes, are significantly enacted; (iv) Sport as a moral force; (v) Sport as celebrating both the life of the body and marking its limitations.

Between 1940 and 1951, *The Pride of the Yankees, Knute Rockne All American, Gentleman Jim* (the boxer James J. Corbett, 1942), and *Jim Thorpe All American* depict non-mainstream Americans (Gehrig the son of German immigrants, Rockne of Norwegian, Corbett of Irish) moving to the centre through sporting prowess. Two of the titles play on the double meaning of 'All American': i.e. selected among the best of the year, and become wholly American out of the melting pot ('don't talk Norwegian, Dad', Rockne as a boy admonishes his old world father, 'we're all Americans now'). Thorpe, a native American, is further outside the dominant culture than the others. Playing the white man's games, he is a median term amongst the first biopics based on black athletes breaking race barriers (*The Joe Louis Story*, 1950, *The Jackie Robinson Story*, 1953). Sport thus is presented as a powerful validation of American social mobility, proving that in America you can choose to be what you want. In *Gentleman Jim*, Corbett's 'scientific' fighting style and social climbing act out not just a refining of what his brawling

The Death of
'The Gipper' in
Knute Rockne

Irish family stand for but a general refining of national manners articulated through his boxing. At the same time these films may overtly bind sport to national moral purposes, as when Rockne defends college football against a hostile educationalist as a channel for male aggression, and a bulwark against American youth going 'soft'. *The Pride of the Yankees* was released soon after the US entered World War Two, and is epigraphed by Damon Runyon's words linking Gehrig's courage in dying to the battlefield fates of young men. This military building of manhood has a more softly patriarchal inflection in the Ruth, Gehrig and Thorpe films' emphasis on the heroes' positive influence on children. In a contradiction fundamental to the meanings of sports, the heroes are seen both as carrying meanings such as the above, and yet also as proponents of pure play divorced from the complex world, though this last is complicated by ambivalences in the part approval/part denigration of the sportsman as childlike encapsulated in Ruth's nickname of 'Babe', in Gehrig's slight slowness as played by Gary Cooper, in Thorpe's difficulties with the adult world, and in Corbett's narcissism.

Lastly, all these films, though optimistic in their thrust, either embrace the realities of death – the ultimate breaking up of the body, e.g. the famous death of 'The Gipper' in *Knute Rockne*, the dying Gehrig walking from the light of Yankee Stadium into darkness – or more usually the little death of the diminution of the sportsman's powers dramatised variously in *The Babe Ruth Story* and *Jim Thorpe*, and most affectingly where Corbett meets the defeated Sullivan at his victory party in *Gentleman Jim*. In the

The Spectre of Defeat:
Sullivan at Corbett's
victory celebration in
Gentleman Jim

golfing biopic, *Follow the Sun*: *The Ben Hogan Story* (1951) the period's rigid lifestory form finds different emphases within basic patterns – rise to fame, comeback after injuries and so on. Here a novel concern is the pressured sportsman's mental fragility, different, say, from Thorpe's problems of racial identity, which precede his sporting life. Hogan's psychological affliction is far from the extreme of the oedipally-incited one mentally unbalancing Jimmy Piersall in *Fear Strikes Out* (1957), the result of his father's pressure on him to succeed at baseball. But *Follow the Sun* and *Fear Strikes Out* both display a psychologising of the sports biopic analogous to the psychologising of other genres of the time, as Hogan struggles against feelings that his nickname of 'the Texas iceberg' demonstrates his inability to be popular, fears only eased by the public response to his courage in resuming his career after a terrible car crash.

Sports biopics continue into the present, negotiating between stubborn inherited idealising structures, too simple and cynical subversions of them, and movements towards more complex engagements with ambivalence, opacity, and the many contemporary meanings of sports. Some significant examples being: *Dawn!*, the swimmer Dawn Fraser; *Raging Bull*, Scorsese's famous take on Jake LaMotta; *Heart Like a Wheel* (Jonathan Kaplan, 1983), the drag racer Shirley Muldowney; *Cobb*, (Ron Shelton, 1994), the baseballer Ty Cobb; *Best* (Mary McGuckian, 2000), the football superstar George Best; and *Ali* (Michael Mann, 2001). Among these, two characteristics depart significantly from tradition, with two films centred on sportswomen, unknown in the classical biopic; and three portraying pathologically self-destructive figures undermining the noble Gehrig paradigm. *Cobb*'s journalist narrator has a more complex role than Sam Blake, *The Pride of the Yankee*'s good newspaperman-celebrant of the hero, faced with the decision, when hired by the dying Cobb to ghost his autobiography, whether to publish Cobb's account, or his own exposé of the legend's viciousness. His 'printing the legend' ironically acknowledges the biopic's – and its audience's – tendency to idealisation. Despite *Raging Bull*'s gospel quotation afterword with its hints of the director's belief in his character's redemption, it is difficult to see Scorsese's Jake LaMotta transcending the paranoia and the violence of which his ring style is only one aspect, as the film pessimistically reworks Rocky Graziano's trajectory in *Somebody Up There Likes Me* (1956) from Barbella to Graziano (barbarism to grace), juvenile death house candidate to domesticated family man, even if still a spectacularly dirty fighter. In *Best* the protagonist, a hedonistic age's literal 'hero of consumption', unbalanced by his new role of sporting pop star, neglects his talent, ultimately the only thing meaningful to him, unrestrainable even by the great manager Matt Busby. *Dawn!*, a downbeat biopic of Dawn Fraser, the 100 metres freestyle winner at three Olympics, evades the classical biopic mould in several ways, in its very Australian interest in the larrikin, the misbehaving nonconformist, in its long post-sporting prominence section portraying the heroine's unsuccessful attempts to find a satisfactory sexual relationship, either heterosexual or lesbian, and in its muted celebration of her inability or refusal to abandon her working class roots. Michael Mann's *Ali*, made in the context of Spike Lee's *Malcolm X*'s (1992) foregrounding of black 1960s politics, belongs to a different age than the 'good negro' heroes of *The Joe Louis Story* and *The Jackie Robinson Story*, whose patient deportment countered the white supremacist's nightmare of Jack Johnson's arrogant 'bad nigger' holding the world heavyweight championship (1908–15). Johnson was himself the subject of a lightly disguised biopic, *The Great White Hope* (Martin Ritt, 1970), made during Ali's persecution for refusing the draft and suggesting links between the two noncompliant champions. *Ali*, though ending traditionally with his regaining his crown by knocking out Foreman, and avoiding as many questions as it answers – almost inevitably with the complexity of the issues surrounding the hero – gives considerable space to the boxer's relationships with Malcolm X, Elijah Muhammad and the Nation of Islam, thus bringing radical racial politics into the sub-genre. While not even gesturing to Ali's Parkinson's Disease-stricken later life (which *When We Were Kings* (Leon Gast and Taylor Hackford, 1996), the documentary of the Kinshasa fight does touch on at its end), the film modulates its celebration of his charisma, importance, and individual and racial self-assertion with complex moments in which he appears, in reiterated shots, silent, pensive, even bewildered, the not-wholly-in-control centre of the many meanings he carries for others.

The sports history film

Every sports film reproduces a historical *zeitgeist*, past or present, or both, as present engages with past, but two of the genre's sub-types engage directly with history – the documentary, dealing with real-world performers and events in a way unmediated by fiction, and the biopic, turning into dramatic form the lives of real sports figures. A third type, here designated the sports history film, differs from the biopic in not centring on a single individual's trajectory, but instead reconstructing a historical sporting event. It also differs from documentary, and parallels the biopic, in combining the appeal to fact with use – certainly with regard to the classical biopic, slightly more restrained use – of the resources of fictional dramatisation.

Some instances are *8 Men Out* (John Sayles, 1988), retelling the 1919 Boston White Sox's throwing of the baseball World Series; *Bodyline* (1984), the Australian television mini-series reconstructing the violent 'Bodyline' England v Australia cricket series of 1932–3; *The Four Minute Mile* (Jim Goddard, 1988), an Anglo Australian two-part television mini-series centring on the rival athletes striving in the early 1950s to run the first sub four minute mile; *Invictus*, retelling the 1995 rugby World Cup; the German film *The Miracle of Bern* (2003), reenacting West Germany's upset defeat of the mighty Hungarians at the 1954 football World Cup; *Miracle at Oxford* (aka *True Blue*, Ferdinand Fairfax, 1996), based on the 1967 Oxford v Cambridge boat race; *When Billie Beat Bobby* (Jane Anderson, 2001), on the tennis challenge between the women's champion Billie Jean King and the old male ex-champion, Bobby Riggs; and *Chariots of Fire* (1981), recounting the victories of the British runners Harold Abrahams and Eric Liddell at the 1924 Paris Olympics. Such films differ from the biopic in various ways. (i) In a marked tendency to have multiple rather than single protagonists – e.g. Bannister, Landy, and Santee in *The Four Minute Mile;* Bradman, Jardine and Larwood in *Bodyline*; the eight ('Shoeless Joe' Jackson, Gandil, Weaver and so on) in *8 Men Out;* Abrahams, Liddell, and the fictional Lord Lindsay in *Chariots of Fire;* both King and Riggs in *When Billie Beat Bobby*. (ii) In eschewing the biopic's typically longer trajectory to highlight one major event, e.g. the England v Australia cricket series of 1932–3, the baseball World Series of 1919, the 2002 baseball season in *Moneyball* (2011), the 1954 football World Cup. *The Four Minute Mile* has a longer chronological span, 1946–54, than the other events (though *Bodyline* stretches from 1928 to 1933 and briefly even further back with scenes from Jardine's and Bradman's childhoods establishing the backstory), but still can be seen as one sustained happening – the competition of the various athletes to break the four minute barrier, with three climaxes, the Englishman Bannister first breaking four minutes, the Australian Landy beating his record, and finally

Bannister beating Landy at the 1954 Empire Games. (iii) The sports history film, with a wider perspective than the biopic, may focus equally on both the opposing teams, or both, or all, of the rivals, in a more totalising gestalt than the biopic's often simple oppositional structures. While this is not a feature of *8 Men Out, The Miracle of Bern, Invictus, Moneyball* and *Chariots of Fire*, it certainly is of *Bodyline* and *The Four Minute Mile*, both films about Anglo-Australian relations and rivalries, necessitating understanding of, and investment in, both sides, and of *When Billie Beat Bobby*. In *The Four Minute Mile*, after Bannister's victory, the English spokesman's banquet speech sees the race's greatness enabled as much by the loser, Landy, as by the winner. (iv) It is also characteristic of these films, all recent, that they tend to be rather more respectful of known facts, the 'discourse of [sports] history' to use Robert Rosenstone's term (Rosenstone, 2006) than biopics, particularly earlier ones. This is because they are the products of a time when a highly developed sports journalism has diffused historical information widely, and where, consequently, factual authenticity has become a value to audiences knowledgeable in sports history. Nevertheless, the difference between the older biopic and the sports history film and certain modern biopics is one of degree rather than essence, since all are ruled by the popular dramatic film's necessary omissions, contractions and shapings of incidents, and assignments of unrecorded motivations and feelings, a truth persuasively articulated by Rosenstone (Rosenstone, 2006).

Did Ring Lardner really walk past the White Sox players in a train singing 'I'm for ever blowing ballgames?' Probably not, but he certainly should have. Did Buck Weaver really recognise Shoeless Joe in the New Jersey minors in 1925? Almost certainly not, but the reason he, rather than an anonymous other, does in the film, is what distinguishes historical drama from history. The analysis of *Chariots of Fire* later in this book notes various inventions altering 'the discourse of history' for purposes of dramatic heightening and concision. Are we shocked that Eric Liddell was never entered for the 1924 100 metres at all because he knew months ahead he would have to run on a Sunday? Unless we think of the sports history film as ruled by the same criteria as Documentary, where such alterations would be unjustifiable, we will probably accede to the argument that finding out he cannot run only days beforehand is justified by its allowing a more dramatic statement of his evangelical Protestant principles.

Two of the nine instances of the sub-type noted were made for television broadcast with a longer time-span than the feature film, which suits (v) its tendency to develop authentic detail, even if alongside invented ones. This detail is often quite specialised, providing pleasure for the knowledgeable sports follower, even if likely to be overlooked by many viewers. For instance, in *The Four Minute Mile*, when Landy competes unsuccessfully at the 1952 Olympics he is encouraged by Marjorie Jackson, the great Australian sprinter, whose presence delights the athletics aficionado, just as the representations of Chris Evert and Margaret Court (though the latter might be thought unfair, even offensive) and mention of Tony Trabert do the same for tennis followers in *When Billie Beat Bobby*.

The women's baseball comedy-drama *A League of Their Own* (Penny Marshall,1992) is an instance that abuts onto the sports history film, but in which precise factuality is downplayed so that, although the war time women's baseball, the Midwest secondary cities base of the All American Girls Baseball League, and the teams' names (e.g 'The Rockford Peaches') reflect reality, no single biographically recognisable person appears, which places it at the margins of a type whose interpretations of history emphasise specific real life participants.

The sports history film proper may adopt one of two time honoured strategies, either inventing 'average' or 'mediocre' characters who are affected by historical events, with the main real life historical characters in the background – Lukác's analysis of Sir Walter Scott's method (Lukács 1969: 32–41), or, as in many historical dramas, placing the major historical characters in the foreground – the latter overwhelmingly the usual procedure, the former followed in only one of the instances discussed here. This, *The Miracle of Bern*, deploys two wholly fictional plots in its account of the West German football team's upsetting of the great Hungarians to win the 1954 football World Cup, the first centred on a troubled, football-loving young boy, Matthias, the second, much slighter, centred on a young journalist and his wife attending the tournament with the wife's conversion from uninterest to enthusiasm suggesting the meaning the victory has for the wider population. *The Miracle of Bern* is one of those films that celebrates sport's ability to positively affect mass feelings in the nation, here a grim post-war West Germany, still shadowed by the disasters of World War Two. Its central fiction exemplifies the psychic difficulties of German life circa 1954, by focusing on the traumatic return of German POWs from

Russia as much as nine years after the war's end, one of them the boy
Matthias' father whose difficulties adjusting create multiple problems. The
intimate connection Matthias has with the World Cup is through Helmut
Rahn of the national team, who lives nearby, with Matthias becoming
Rahn's mascot, and Rahn his father substitute, a situation with which the
alienated father has to come to terms. As the German team moves through
the tournament with unexpected success, the narrative cuts between the
coach Sepp Herberger and his team in Bern and the family, with Matthias'
father finally bonding with the boy by taking him to the final, where his
presence inspires Rahn's winning goal. This, of course, is fiction, but the
following of the team's progress is factual, with the win in the final facili-
tated by rain, to the more skilful Hungarians' disadvantage, and by the
German team's new studs, developed to handle such conditions. *8 Men
Out*, by contrast, eschews overt fictionalisation on the scale of *The Miracle*,
restricting its dramatisation to the historical actants and interpretation of
their actions and motives – the eight, the manager Comiskey, the gangster Rothstein, the sports writer Ring Lardner, the Baseball Commissioner
Judge Landis and so on. On the other hand, its treatment of a scandal mas-
sively investigated over ninety years is telescoped, for instance with no
indication that the players played the 1920 season before being banned,
and selective, choosing to make Weaver, probably the least compromised
of the players, a focal point, thus producing a compelling interpretation of
the material rather than an impossible window onto absolute truth. *When
Billie Beat Bobbie* can be seen as a paradigm of the difficulties of reconstructing ideologically contentious history in its being almost two separate
films, one rather stridently presenting King as a major feminist icon, the
other – more centred on Riggs – emphasising the comic grotesque aspects
of a challenge match more media circus than meaningful sport or sexual
politics.

The sports documentary

The sports documentary film exhibits two basic impulses: one, derived
from Eadweard Muybridge's analytical stop motion photography of bodies
in action (*Animal Locomotion*, 1887, and *The Human Figure in Motion*,
1901), leading to the delineation and celebration of sporting motion: the
other pursuing the social meanings of sporting phenomena – played and

watched where, by whom, under what conditions, with what meanings? The distinction is theoretically useful, but blurs in practice, where the separate impulses merge, so that films seemingly treating sport as pure activity cannot help touching on social meanings, while films undertaking sociological investigation can seldom resist embodying sport's lyrical, ludic dimension. The recent *Zidane a Twentyfirst Century Portrait* (2006), might seem an extreme of the former, centred almost wholly on the footballer in real-time action, to the seeming exclusion of all else, but not only is this obsessive visual concentration complicated by the player's gnomic reflections, but at half time a montage of global news items (a marathon reading of *Don Quixote* for its 400th anniversary, a car bomb in Iraq) linked only by their coinciding with the game's 23 April 2007 date, interacts with the film's football images. Conversely, another well-known documentary, *Hoop Dreams* (1993), follows two black Chicago male adolescents for more than two years as they attempt, not very successfully, to make it through the college basketball scholarship system to the pinnacle of an NBA team, against great odds (even though 80% of NBA players are Afro-American), dysfunctional fathers, poverty, crime, drugs and the blandishments of a scholarship system promising more than it gives. For all that the sport is the centre of a systemic commercial world spreading through the educational system, blocking off alternative possibilities to young black men, the school and college games shown celebrate the sport's aesthetic and kinetic quiddity.

The most prominent sports documentary sub-types include factual biographies (as distinct from biopics, e.g. the recent highly praised *Senna*, Asif Kapadia, 2010), histories of sports (e.g. Ken Burns' *Baseball*, 1994, with its twelve television episodes), coverage of major events (e.g. *When We Were Kings*, the Ali Foreman fight), and the looser category of the essay (e.g. the French Canadian Giles Groulx's short boxing and ice hockey films *Golden Gloves*, 1961, and *Un Jeu Si Simple*, 1964, the New Zealander Florian Habicht's *Kaikohe Demolition*, 2004, and Louis Malle's *Vive Le Tour!*, 1962). These categories are not exhaustive, as *Trobriand Cricket: An Ingenious Response to Colonialism* (Gary Kildea and Jerry Leach, 1979) shows, an anthropological documentary recording the metamorphoses the game, introduced by Australian missionaries, underwent in a place where local needs were unsupervised by international regulation and competition. Jean Vigo's *La Natation par Jean Taris* (1931) – Jean Taris being a French swimming champion – is a curiosity, a kind of parody instruction film with trick effects, possibly owing its existence to Vigo's desire to experiment with water and underwater photography, important to his later masterpiece *L'Atalante* (1934).

Like other members of the wider genre, sports documentaries, however categorised, can be seen moving between tendencies persuasively defined as the Poetic, Expository, Observational, Participatory, Reflexive and Performative (Bill Nichols 2001: 99–138). In that most sports documentaries are largely dominated by tendencies 2 (with its typical explaining/celebrating voice over), 3 (with its fly on the wall characteristics), and 4 (with its talking heads and interviews), but show little input from 5 and 6, we can define in general a formally rather conservative mode, the most radical elements of which most often occur where the 'poetry of motion' (a version of category 1) is foregrounded, pushing towards the art film.

Like all documentaries, sports documentaries succeed by showing reality in a new light, thus prompting a more particular or wider understanding, as two cycling documentaries demonstrate. Louis Malle's short *Vive Le Tour!* typifies the essay film's loose structure, delineating many things – the crowds of all ages, including priests and nuns, enjoying a *fête* as they watch the Tour de France pass through small towns and villages, the functions of the fleets of following cars interweaving with, but seemingly never crashing into, the riders, the vital matter of food and drink for the contestants, and the curse of drug-taking in professional cycling. The feature length Danish film *A Sunday in Hell/En Forasdag i Helvede* (Jørgen Leth, 1977), has a more orthodox linear structure, closely following the chief contestants in the gruelling Paris-Roubaix race, its dominant voice over explaining which riders are most suited to the hazardous course, but also emphasising the event's commercial underpinnings – the riders encountering a demonstration against a sponsor, the winner having to drink a particular mineral water on the victory podium. Two particular micro moments demonstrate the documentarist's ability to reveal the overlooked or taken for granted: (i) the opening where a competitor delicately brushes with what looks like a shaving brush the wheel spokes and chains of a racing bike highlighting its mixture of the steely tensile and delicately fragile; (ii) the cycling star De Vlaminck's pre-race massage revealing his legs' distended musculature caused by the specialised physical activity of cycle racing.

A well-known documentary that crosses a number of the categories listed above, but eschews the conventional voice over for a polyphony of voices is *When We Were Kings*, centred around the heavyweight championship fight in Kinshasa in which Muhammed Ali defeated George Foreman. It has built into it complex retrospective and multi-layered elements, due to its basic footage, shot by Gast at the time of the fight and the accompanying Afro-American music festival (featuring James Brown, B.B.King and others), being abandoned, then two decades afterwards intricately combined with both later and earlier footage by Hackford. The resulting 1970s/1990s palimpsest is composed of the original footage of the build-up to the fight in the dictator Mobutu's Zaire, the promoter Don King's epic hustling, Ali and Foreman's press conferences, the fighters training, musical performances, and the remarkable fight itself, combined with archive footage of Lumumba's fall and Mobutu's rise in the Congo crisis, civil rights protests and violence in the US, the rise of Black Power and Clay/Ali's ascent to fame. Additionally, cultural commentators, including Norman Mailer, George Plimpton and Spike Lee, discuss the fight's and Ali's significance. The combination of original footage, archive material, and later commentary reliving the fight and its meanings, makes for a complex, intricately structured film, dealing not just with fact but the cultural desires and fantasies of two different eras for whom the events have significance.

No account of the subgenre should omit the most famous of all sports documentaries, Leni Riefenstahl's film of the 1936 Berlin Olympics, *Olympia* (1938), with its extreme dramatisation of the intersection of sporting and ideological meanings. The film is undoubtedly revolutionary in its technical brilliance in the handling of sports action, but while the imagination that conceived it was entranced by the athletic body (erotically entranced too as the director's affair with one of the athletes most foregrounded in the film, the American decathlete, Glen Morris, attests, with the athlete given a triumphal imaging none of the German winners is granted, his laurel-crowned head superimposed on the national flag), its concrete realisation was only possible through the extraordinary state resources put at the director's disposal, which, though more discreetly and ambiguously than in Riefenstahl's celebration of the 1934 Nuremburg Rally, *The Triumph of the Will* (1935), ultimately glorified the Nazi State. One has only to compare the footage in the forgotten 1948 London Games

Towards the condition
of art, in *Olympia*

film of Fanny Blankers-Koen gaining her celebrated victories in undramatic longshot, to see how far ahead *Olympia* was with its innovations – the rail-propelled camera racing alongside the sprinters, events replayed from multiple angles, the deployment of telescopic lenses, slow motion and multiple camera positions for the most dramatic and revealing shots possible, particularly in the jumping and diving events. The glorification of the (Aryan) body was fundamental to Nazi ideology, malign in its attitudes towards the perceived defective body of the racial other, lending an uneasiness to the otherwise magical celebration of nature at the beginning of Part 2's 'Festival of Beauty' when the naked athletes (soldiers?) run through the forest into the lake. But the celebration of bodily beauty and athletic endeavour hardly necessarily denote fascism, though they are clearly open to appropriation by it. To do Riefenstahl's film justice, in a way that never exists in *Triumph of the Will*, distance between the film's ideology of bodily celebration and National Socialist appropriations, between the Olympian dedication 'to the glory and honour of youth' and the Nazi cult of youth is present. This is most obvious in the positive visualisation of non-Aryan athletes, most notably the great Afro-American sprinter and long jumper Jesse Owens whose 'black mercenary' victories angered Hitler, but are a highlight of the film. Susan Sontag's famous essay 'Fascinating Fascism' which undermines mythologies of Riefenstahl's claimed detachment from Nazism, admits, 'in matters of beauty, she is not racist' (1983: 317). And, though no doubt encouraged by the successes of German women athletes, the film spends more time with female competitors (as distinct from massed eurythmicists) than might be expected, given the Nazi valuation of women as primarily breeders, another point at which Riefensthal's bodily interests are not identical with the regime's. The prologue is a prime instance of the ambiguity which haunts the film, with its tropes in which antique Greek statues of perfect male and female forms come to life, with the statue 'Discobolus' metamorphosing into the living form of the German decathlete, Huber. This is followed by the running of the torch from Olympus to the host city, a ritual invented for Berlin by Karl Diem, which, like the trope of the vivified sculptures, is designed to be interpreted as the fulfilment of classical Greek ideals in the modern Games (and has been, despite its origins, included in Olympic opening rituals ever since), but also in Nazi Germany, with the descent from the clouds over Nuremburg in *Triumph of the Will* echoed in the movement through clouds to the Olympic stadium. And just as the pattern of searchlights (based on Albert Speer's stadium spectacle) which closes the film suggests the future furies of aerial bombardment, so there are inevitable retrospective ironies in the route traced on maps and superimposed images ('Griechenland, Bulgarien, Jugoslavien, Ungarn, Österreich, Tschetschoslovakien, Deutschland') which it is hard not to see foreshadowing Nazi European conquests, a contagion touching highly militarised areas, like the modern pentathlon and the equestrian events, and the use of replica human targets in one of the shooting events. However read, some of these sequences are constructed out of a mixture of real-time coverage, special effects photography and creative editing, which alerts us to the fact that documentary is not restricted to live shooting but may create effects and arguments through artifice. Though much of the film depends on a sense of really being there, Riefenstahl reshot certain sequences (e.g. the decathlon 1500 metres, the end of the pole vault, the brief but spectacular yachting sequences with the cameras on board that were not allowed in the actual competition) and interpolated material, as in the marathon segment, where there are subjective shots of the road and runners' feet clearly taken outside the race, and at one point a bare torsoed black man running.

Where in documentaries the observation/celebration of bodies in motion pushes to the margins the usual predominant material of results, victories, technical analyses, 'human interest' stories, the social meanings of sport and so on, they sometimes move in the direction of the art film, as can be seen in the Olympic documentaries by Riefenstahl and Kon Ichikawa (*Tokyo Olympiad*, 1965). The Olympic film as a recognisable sports documentary sub-type has two overriding constraints, first to record the drama and winners of the major events; second to celebrate, as well as the international Olympic ideal, or what remains of it, the nation and city staging the games. Other Olympic films are largely unremembered, having little appeal beyond being records of the past, a not inconsiderable virtue, of course; this writer having several times replayed *Olympia* just to revisit Jack Lovelock winning the 1500 metres. Both Riefenstahl's and Ichikawa's films have many passages defined by these constraints. The first half of *Olympia*, largely devoted to the athletics competitions, follows many events in an orthodox way, and in the second half the brief coverage of team events like the hockey, football and polo is largely conventional. But at various points the film moves towards lyrical abstraction – e.g. the pole vaulting sequence with vaulter succeeding vaulter, until they become silhouettes against the darkening sky, without commentary of any kind; or the fencing sequence which begins like shadow puppetry with the action at first given through the battling shadows to which at screen top or bottom the competitors' feet (all of their bodies that are visible) are attached, and most famously the men's high diving which becomes a completely deindividualised celebration of form and motion, created on the editing table. Ichikawa's *Tokyo Olympiad*, though apparently disliked by the Japanese Olympic Committee for not doing enough of the obvious, certainly follows convention at points, particularly in the extended coverage of the Japan vs USSR women's volleyball final, with its obvious nationalist appeal. Elsewhere, however, it pushes the conventional international and national assertions into a historically conscious and meditative mode, underlining the coming of the games to Asia, as distinct from Japan only, marking the growing African participation, and, in an instance of significant documentary intertextuality, reworking Riefenstahl's descent through the clouds to Berlin with a mirror moment above Hiroshima. Departing from the usual concentration on victors, *Tokyo Olympiad* exhibits interest in losers, and like *Olympia*, with which it clearly seeks comparison, also moves to lyric abstraction, in a number of sequences essaying formal experiments – e.g. the women's fencing sequence which refuses establishing shots and shows only fragmented parts, and the canoeing which is more interested in the play of light on water than the event. An unofficial film of the 1972

Munich Olympics, the multiple-authored *Visions of Eight* (1973), exaggerates Riefenstahl's and Ichikawa's departures from orthodox recording into a film made up of eight separate short films by film-makers on subjects of their choosing – 'the strongest', i.e. weightlifting, by Mai Zetterling, 'the highest', i.e. pole vaulting, by Arthur Penn, the female competitors by Michael Pfleghar, the decathlon by Milos Forman, the losers by Claude Lelouch, resulting in personalised essayistic films, amongst the many themes of which the loneliness and isolation (typical art film motifs) of the athlete are often predominant.

The boxing film

Of the sub-types based on particular sports, the boxing film most demands coverage, for reasons of both quantity and quality, and because, allowing for hyperbole's irresponsible attractions, there is still a grain of truth in the claim 'that it was boxing that created cinema' (McKernan 1996: 107). An expert in the sub-genre's early history claims over 100 fight films by 1907 and more than 200 by 1915, explaining that 'Boxing, with its brief rounds confined to a single setting, was highly compatible with early film-making, with its limited length of celluloid and restricted camera movement' (Streibel 2008: 17–18). Further, the first feature length film was Enoch Rector's filming of the 1897 Corbett-Fitzsimmons bout. These were 'actualities', recordings of real fights (or cheap reconstructions cashing in on them), but fictions followed and boxing became easily the most prolific sports subject, with Zucker and Babich's 1987 listing of 446 compared with 119 for baseball and 289 for horse racing (and other equestrian sports). This preeminence is also qualitative, with films such as *Raging Bull*, *Fat City*, *Body and Soul* (Robert Rossen, 1947) and *Million Dollar Baby* (Clint Eastwood, 2004) widely judged to be major works.

Why so many memorable boxing films? And literary works (Hazlitt, Jack London, Hemingway, Mailer, A. J. Liebling and so on)? Whether literary or cinematic, the sub-genre has inbuilt characteristics. First, of all sports, boxing fascinates as the most violent. Second, in a genre often superficially optimistic it is the closest to tragic. Diana's coach, Hector, in *Girlfight* (Karyn Kusama, 2001) replies when asked about his career, 'What happened to most of us who do it ... we lose.' Typically boxers like 'Kid' Curtis, who dies, ironically, after winning his fight in *The Square Ring*

(Basil Dearden and Michael Relph, 1953), keep going by fantasising about a last big payday. In *The Set-Up* (Robert Wise, 1949) the ageing Stoker Thompson's hopes are parodied by the obsession of the pathetically declining 'Gunboat' with Frankie Manila, who, though beaten 21 times, became world champion in an upset. When 'Gunboat', returned from the ring semi-comatose, is asked his name by the doctor, he replies, 'Frankie Manila, Champion of the World'.

Second, every athlete faces the moment of the perfected body's disintegration, but the boxer faces it most irrevocably. Further, the 'punchie' is a recurring character in boxing films, a brain-damaged reminder of the sport as 'a one way ticket to Palookaville' (Terry Molloy/Marlon Brando in *On the Waterfront*, Elia Kazan, 1954). Third, as traditional underclass escape route, it is the sport most closely connected with ethnic and class struggle (in America the Irish, Italians, Jews, Latinos and, of course, Afro-Americans, with the meanings that Jack Johnson, Joe Louis and Muhammed Ali held for disempowered Afro-Americans much documented), its violence making it an exemplar of social conflict and Social Darwinism. Fourth, of all sports, it has the closest connection to organised crime, with fight fixing driven by gambling almost as recurrent in real life as in fiction. But fifth, outweighing such negatives, the fighter's existential dare possesses an aura of heroism celebrated by intellectuals from Hazlitt to Mailer and Joyce Carol Oates, so that there is, even when boxing seems in decline, especially in America, no end to the stories that it generates (Boddy 2008, 391).

Boxing films basically divide into two opposing categories: in one corner the boxer as victim, in the other as hero. Two well-known films' ambiguous titles dramatise this. *Body and Soul* reads negatively as Body endangering Soul, underlined by the strenuous antinomies set up between injuring (even killing) opponents and fighting for civilised values in that film – particularly when the persecution of the Jewish protagonist's co-religionists is mentioned. In *Golden Boy* (Rouben Mamoulian, 1939) Joe Bonaparte is torn between talents for the ring and the violin. But in films like *Rocky* and *Ali*, and the Korean *Champion*/*Hangui* (Kyung-Taek Kwak, 2002) and *Crying Fist*/*Jumeogi Unda* (Ryu Seung-Wan, 2005) body and soul are indissoluble, the body's activity soulful, boxing a heroic undertaking. The title *Golden Boy* may be ironic in Odets's play and Mamoulian's adaptation (as the boxer, like the *ingénu* gangster, enjoys luxurious trappings and expensive women), but in the affirmative boxing film it is a gold-leafed metaphor for heroic, even spiritual triumph. The negative category includes *The Set-Up*, *Requiem for a Heavyweight*, *Golden Boy*, *Champion* (Mark Robson, 1949), *Body and Soul*, *The Harder They Fall* and *Raging Bull*. The positive, *Gentleman Jim*, *Somebody Up There Likes Me* (Robert Wise, 1956), *Cinderella Man* (Ron Howard, 2005), *Ali*, *Million Dollar Baby*, *Girlfight*, and the two South Korean films *Champion* and *Crying Fist*.

In the first category the boxer is trapped in a system controlled by gangsters, cheating managers, bloodthirsty fans and, insinuated behind them, a harsh economic system in which boxers take out their anger with the system on the opponent in front of them (Oates 1987: 63). The most pathetic victims are *Requiem for a Heavyweight*'s 'Mountain' Rivera and *The Harder They Fall*'s Toro Morino, with the once formidable 'Mountain' forced to fight on well past decline, and then, when retired on medical insistence, pushed into the ignominy of pro wrestling. Toro Morino, a naïve talentless giant, moves through fixed fights towards a title bout (echoing Primo Carnera's handlers' relations with the gangster Owney Madden in the 1930s) only to take a merciless beating from an unbribed opponent, and end duped of the fortune he has made for others. *The Harder They Fall*, related to the social problem exposé film of its time, moves to outright condemnation as the corrupted ex-reporter (Humphrey Bogart), repenting his complicity in Toro's fraudulent rise, ends the film beginning a newspaper article demanding boxing's abolition.

In such films callousness prevails. When the black boxer Ben Chaplin dies as a result of being pressured to fight the hero even though he is carrying a neural injury in *Body and Soul,* the hero's criminal manager merely says 'Everybody dies'. Fight fixing is ubiquitous. In *On the Waterfront,* Terry famously blames his brother for agreeing a fix when 'I coulda been a contender'. In *Raging Bull* Jake 'flip-flops' to get a later title shot. The whole of *The Set-Up* revolves around a fix; 1940s and 1950s boxing films with their emphasis on criminality, trapped and self-entrapped protagonists and the pitiless city, often allude to film noir. In *Champion*'s opening Midge Kelly's entourage walks through the tunnel to the ring in darkness and extreme *chiaroscuro*, the dark broken by pools of light thrown from above, images, which like *Body and Soul*'s opening, announce atmospheric affiliations. In a conceit transferred from film to film the ring at the centre of the empty stadium becomes a literal rather than implicit site of gangsterdom, as individuals who have transgressed against the mob are pursued into it and beaten up – Mountain's manager in *Requiem for a Heavyweight*, Midge Kelly in *The Champion*, Stoker Thompson in *The Set-Up* seemingly trapped in the empty stadium by thugs, though on that occasion they are evaded. In all these instances boxing is a vivid metaphor for the pitiless lower order struggles of the American City (and foreign cities too, e.g. Milan in Visconti's *Rocco and His Brothers* where three of the brothers box for a living).

One way the fighter has of refusing victimhood is winning the fight he is meant to lose, in spite of the consequences – for example, broken hands for Stoker ending his career in *The Set-Up*. At *Body and Soul*'s conclusion Charlie walks past his threatening gangster-manager, announcing his retirement. A disagreement between director (Robert Rossen) and screenwriter (Abraham Polonsky) is recorded, with Rossen wanting Charlie executed by the gangsters, but Polonsky's perhaps surprisingly affirmative closure prevailed, as in Mamoulian's *Golden Boy*, which replaces the play's ending where Joe, now seeking thrills through speed, dies offstage in a car crash, with a sentiment-filled return to home, family and violin. Such closures, like Stoker's wife's vision of a normal life when he can no longer fight, Joe's refusal to be intimidated by the gangster Eddie Fuseli in *Golden Boy*, and Eddie's sending Toro home with his own share of the money in *The Harder They Fall*, soften the narratives briefly, but the boxing world portrayed throughout is bleak. Nowhere more is this the case than in *Champion* where Midge Kelly is the destroyer self-destroyed, a figure who otherwise might belong to the heroic film, battling from poverty to glory, refusing to throw a fight, but consumed by selfishness, betraying those around him, and after his last triumphant win dying of a cerebral haemorrhage.

Slumped in his corner, bruised and bloodied, the fighter recalls the suffering bodies of the martyred saints, even Christ, potential analogies

The boxer's martyred
body in *Raging Bull*

made plain in Scorsese's *Raging Bull,* images bridging the affirmative and negative variants, binding together the protagonists whether victims or heroes. In the affirmative variant where boxing is a heroic existential enterprise, corruption plays little or no part. In the South Korean *Champion* Kim Deuk Gu's manager-coach is so honest that he refuses compensation for a cancelled fight, and makes a contract simply by shaking hands since he believes no ex-boxer would cheat a colleague. The ring is certainly dangerous – Maggie in *Million Dollar Baby* is paralysed and Kim Deuk Gu dies in it, but it is seen as a place of fulfilment particularly for those whose environments offer few positives. Maggie, from 'between goodbye and nowhere', says in *Million Dollar Baby* 'this is the only thing I ever felt good doing'. And Scrap, the film's elderly ex-boxer narrator, explains that boxing is not simply the violence the crowd thinks it wants, but 'about respect' and deals with Maggie's fate by saying 'People die every day, Frankie, mopping floors, washing dishes, and you know what their last thought is? I never got my shot. Because of you Maggie got her shot.' Kim Deuk Gu dies fighting, but the treatment of ring death is wholly different from that in the first set of films where it results from an unscrupulous owner's or manager's callousness. Here it is accepted as the ultimate heroic risk.

An often invoked defence of boxing – that its legitimised violence exorcises otherwise immitigable antisocial violence – has its culminating statement in the Rocky Graziano biopic, *Somebody Up There Likes Me.* *Cinderella Man* (the James J. Braddock biopic) is a late variant on the traditional lower class ascent through boxing, here for its Irish American hero following in the wake of the Italian-American *Rocky* cycle (1976–2006) whose specificities suggest a fantasy of American white working class assertion against perceived disenfranchisement by a multicultural society. This has been plausibly related to the dominance of non-whites in frontline US sports and of blacks in heavyweight boxing where – apart briefly from Johansson, the Swede – there had not been a white titleholder since Rocky Marciano (whom Rocky Balboa clearly recalls) retired undefeated in 1955.

Some Asian boxing films

In South Korea, the Philippines, Japan and Thailand boxing is a major sport, with Olympic and world champions in the lower weight divisions. Two Korean films, *Champion* and *Crying Fist*, parallel the affirmative American films' rise to glory and boxing as social salvation tropes, but also embody major differences. In both, boxing rescues the protagonists. Kim Deuk Gu in the biopic *Champion* says that without boxing he would have been a criminal, and in *Crying Fist* learning boxing in prison redeems the younger man and returning to it gives self-respect to the older man, a despairing ex-Olympic boxer who scratches an abysmal living as a human punchbag on whom passers-by pay to vent their anger. *Crying Fist's* double narrative breaks the individualistic Hollywood pattern by making it almost impossible to favour one boxer over the other when they fight. Further differences from the American prototype are found in the films' communal gyms and training camps (also true of the Thai film *Beautiful Boxer*) under the guidance of a coach whose Zen Master-like authority extends in *Champion* to brutal beatings for those who disappoint, but also to civilising demands (Kim Deuk Gu's mentor's ban on swearing and insistence that he improves his handwriting). In *Beautiful Boxer* the bond between Chaat the manager and Toom the transvestite boxer is so close that, after Chaat's death, there is a subjective sequence mid-fight in which Toom leaves the ring to speak with him. Boxing is not seen as simply violence, but as mind/body discipline. In *Champion* Kim Deuk Gu's ocean-side upbringing suggests it is a vehicle of transcendence when he tells his home villagers that the mind of man must seek to become like an ocean. His ring death is elided into a camera move up to the sky, then down to the beach where the protagonist as a boy lies contemplating the sea. Here, death in the ring is tragic (in an affecting scene his Christian wife dreams his return to her protesting that he is alive and she feels his body, overcoming her doubts, only to wake and see his death reported on TV), but it is the noble gamble the fighter takes, and the film ends years later with the coach bringing Kim Deuk Gu's son to the gym where he sees his father's smiling ghost, and may continue the tradition.

The female boxer

Given the absolute identification of boxing with masculinity, the boxing film's latest narrative enacted in *Girlfight* and *Million Dollar Baby* is particularly contentious, troubling deeply-held ideologies of masculinity and femininity, with the girl boxer's aggression undermining expectations of the nurturing female. Whether female boxing's inclusion in the 2012

Olympics reflects a large-scale shift in cultural attitudes is unclear, but certainly, in her filmic existence, the girl boxer has become a symbolic figure of freedom from gender prohibitions. What reactions Hilary Swank in *Million Dollar Baby* and Michelle Rodriguez in *Girlfight* arouse in male and female audiences is difficult to speculate, but clearly the films intend to elicit feelings different from traditional male voyeuristic interest. While vindicating their heroines' choices, the films also develop plots of emotional intimacy demonstrating that possessing 'masculine' traits does not necessarily mean the disappearance of 'feminine' ones, as witness the fatherly-daughterly love between Maggie and her aged mentors (Clint Eastwood and Morgan Freeman). Though Diana in *Girlfight* literally fights her father and defeats her boyfriend in the ring, the film shows her in love with the latter. In *Girlfight* the amateur championship in which Diana defeats her boyfriend is 'gender blind', i.e. female against male at the same weight, the film's invention since there has only been one sanctioned mixed bout in the US, in Seattle in 1999, overwhelmingly regarded as farcically distasteful, underlining the film's fight as symbolic fiction. An interesting variation on masculinities, femininities and boxing, in this case Muay Thai (Thai kickboxing), is enacted in the Thai film *Beautiful Boxer* where the highly feminised hero uses his boxing talents professionally to care for his family, then to fund the sex change operation he has desired since childhood.

Fat City

John Huston's *Fat City* evades the twin categories most boxing films fall into, and the usual hero/victim antithesis. Set largely in the desolation of Stockton, California, its boxers operate in small-time settings, far from the razzle-dazzle of contendership. Like the Korean *Crying Fist* it has double protagonists, the older ex-pro Billy Tully (Stacey Keach) and the younger novice Eddie (Jeff Bridges), both talented but unlikely ever to make it to the 'fat city' of the ordinary boxer's dreams, not because of bribery or corruption but just luck and accident. In this film boxing is a hard lower class occupation like the poorly paid agricultural labour the boxers undertake when not active. When Billy's manager, Ruben Luna, gives him only $100 of a $200 purse, Ruben's accounting seems honest and like the others, he has to make a living for himself and his family. An understated sympathy and respect, without sentimentalising or existential aggrandising of the sport, runs through the film, extending to the lonely figure of another fighter, Lucero, pissing blood in the hotel before his fight with Billy, and leaving the stadium alone, defeated.

2   DOMINANT PRESENCES: TWO

Spectacle and the sports film

Like the epic, the musical, and the war film, the sports film highlights particular spectacles, namely bodies in motion in rulebound contests, as distinct
from song and dance or the choreography of combat. These vary from the
minimal in a surprising number of films, including the recent, highly pub-
licised *Moneyball* (Bennett Miller, 2011), to *Lagaan*'s encounter, which is
more than an hour long. Action sequences in most films fall between these
extremes, the most minimal underlining the rule that action sequences,
however necessary, however much criticised if unconvincing, are not in
themselves the genre's essence. Though judged in large part against
canons of verisimilitude derived from watching sport, predominantly, since
the early 1950s, on TV, these replica sporting spectacles are fundamentally
distinguished (i) by their reduction of events to dramatic highlights (except
with events of the shortest duration like the 100 metres in *Chariots of Fire*
where they may be expanded rather than contracted, by slow motion and
replays); (ii) by their connection to a surrounding dramatic narrative; and
(iii) by their overt deployment of visual and sonic rhetoric, especially the
presence of music (true, but to a more limited degree of the sports action
in documentaries), to surround the representations with emotional force in
the absence of the uncertainty and other emotive factors surrounding real
world sports events.

Media developments have created pressures on the spectacle in contemporary sports films hardly known before bigger screen, colour, higher definition television sports coverage with multiple cameras, extreme close-ups and hyper slow motion replay increased film viewers' expectations. Most audiences before the early 1950s, having seen real life sports on screen only in newsreels, would have been less demanding as regards verisimilitude, accepting the stock footage of unrelated baseball or football games with staged close-ups added typical of older biopics.

Each sports subject has its own potential for visual and sonic spectacle. John Frankenheimer's *Grand Prix* (1962) utilised Cinerama's enormous screen, cameras attached to the cars and filming from helicopters, to create kinetic excitement. At times, though, its spectacle moves from augmented visual and sonic hyperrealism into extraordinary artificial patternings, with the giant screen dividing into grids combining up to 32 images. In the French Grand Prix sequence images of cars shot through telescopic lenses are edited into dancelike arrangements recalling the work of Busby Berkeley. In extreme contrast to *Grand Prix*'s capturing of speed is the slow intense play in the pool film's confined space. *The Color of Money* (Martin Scorsese, 1986) is by the director's standards statically shot, but the pool sequences explosively release the dynamism frustrated elsewhere – the camera low on the table swooping in travelling shots alongside or behind the struck ball, or shooting forward to register the hyperbolic shocks of the collision of cue on ball, then ball on ball. Various aquatic sports, swimming and diving with their underwater shots, and surfing where huge breakers curl over athletes suddenly rendered precarious and diminutive, have their own elemental differences, as do the ice and snow environments of skiing and skating films. That obvious site of spectacle, the boxing film, follows two routes, the first pursuing objectively realistic representations of fighting, the second seeking a subjective registration of combat's shock. Kasia Boddy notes that in Scorsese's *Raging Bull*, against rapid temporal shifts from 24 to 96 frames per second within single shots 'the choreographic rhythm of the fight is created by a soundtrack of photographers' exploding flashbulbs and powerfully amplified punches which not only acts like 'scoring music' to what we see but makes it even more surreal and abstract, effects also imitating those of the stroboscopically lit 1940s (1/3000th –1/300,000th of a second) images of the tabloid photographers Wegee and Charles Hoff' (Boddy 2008: 362). For *Champion*, James Wong Howe shot the fights inside the ring on rollerskates with a handheld camera, with blurring of focus augmenting the sense of realism (Baker 2003: 117). By contrast, in the *Rocky* films comic book violence supplants realism with the fights taking place in a realm of fantastic hyper-kinetic excess.

Staging sports action

The modes of staging sports action in non-documentary films can be simplified to three alternatives:

(1) Simulation by actors.
(2) Use of film or TV actuality footage alone.
(3) The combination of simulated sequences and actuality footage.
Of these (1) and (3) are the dominant modes, with (2) less frequent.

(1) Simulated sequences are obviously easier to stage in films portraying recreational players with only basic skills – e.g. the pub competition rugby league footballers in *Up'n'Under* (John Godber, 1998), the recreational cricketers in *Playing Away* (Horace Ové, 1987), where the problems of actors impersonating highly-skilled sportsmen are avoided, the basic requirement being actors with some minor aptitude for the game. Even so, the recreational ice hockey comedy, *Les Boys* (Louis Saia, 1997), given the skating skills and hyper-physical nature of the sport, has to involve *'doubles de jouers'*. When the action simulates high-level performance, successful representation depends upon camerawork and editing operating on actors capable of representing sports performers convincingly in limited, carefully arranged circumstances. Ian Charleson's Eric Liddell in *Chariots of Fire* might be seen as the epitome of this, broadly incorporating known characteristics of Liddell's running style.

Simulating individual events is simpler than team events where more intricate choreography is demanded. In *Escape to Victory* (John Huston, 1981) some real football stars, notably Pelé, are cast as actors to heighten the game sequences' verisimilitude as well as to attract fan audiences, but this solution to one problem can create two others: (i) most sports stars' lack of acting ability compared with the other actors, and (ii) their onfield skills showing up the actors' sporting inabilities. In *Any Given Sunday,* a film with a lot of simulated play which has to reach high levels of perceived authenticity, the problems are solved by having professional players who have no place in the narrative sequences provide the convincing American football action into which the actors are carefully fitted, the situation also in *Old Scores* where retired rugby stars such as Waka Nathan and Barry John have roles confined to the game. In *Any Given Sunday* the importation of the sports star's aura is achieved without the problems noted above by the use in the narrative of ex-players – Jim Brown and Lawrence Taylor – who have moved from one celebrity field, sport, to another, acting. (An exceptional case is that of *The Jackie Robinson Story*, in which the subject, still in mid-career, plays himself surprisingly effectively, with the bonus of a display of his actual playing skills).

The boxing film is the epitome of realistic, expressionist-tinged simulation, with actors in well-publicised cases painfully acquiring boxing techniques e.g. the many rounds boxed by De Niro training for his role as Jake LaMotta in *Raging Bull*, and by Will Smith for *Ali*, the latter involving detailed mimicking of Ali's characteristics which are so well-known from television. It was much easier in *Gentleman Jim* for Errol Flynn to represent very broadly James J. Corbett's new 'scientific' method and for Ward Bond to imitate John L. Sullivan's older brawling style because audiences were not familiar with them from television, as they certainly were with Ali. In the Hindi women's (field) hockey film *Chak De India!* there is a fair amount of playing that has to convince as high level, managed with some of the cast being hockey players, but with others, non-players, training for six months to create believable action. Robert Towne's *Personal Best* (1982) is a one-off instance of extreme profilmic verisimilitude, with the athlete characters played by competitors of Olympic trial standard, including one of the two protagonists, Patrice Donnelly, with only Mariel Hemingway, the co-protagonist, not a real athlete, though she trained for a year to look highly plausible beside the actual ones. *Personal Best* could thus claim to be the most athletically realistic sports fiction, though inasmuch as few would place it as the best, it provokes the question whether for most audiences there is much perceived difference between the fabricated performances in *Chariots of Fire* and the largely unmediated ones in *Personal Best* and, even if differences are registered, whether they count for much, once a certain point of verisimilitude (the threshold of which has certainly been raised in contemporary films) is reached.

In mode (3) actuality footage is merged with simulation, a strategy largely reserved for sub-types referencing biographical actuality, the biopic and the sports history film. In a rather primitive example, in *The Joe Louis Story* archive fragments of Louis's real bouts are shown, but in long shot so as not to clash with the actor (Coley Wallace) impersonating him, the lack of close action unacceptable in later productions. Made nearly forty years later, *The Four Minute Mile* illustrates a more complex integration in its reconstruction of the Vancouver Empire Games mile, using original footage of Bannister and Landy mixed with closer shots of the actors impersonating them. Two football films, *The Damned United* (Tom Hooper, 2009) and *Best*, are later examples of actuality footage combined with actors impersonating the players on and off the pitch, with the action sequences in *Best* based on close simulation of archive sequences, matched with television archive material. *Grand Prix* provides examples outside the biographical and historical categories, where shots of James Garner and other actors driving smaller versions of the racing cars are intercut with real race footage. This is essentially the same strategy used in early biopics, but with an enormous increase in sophistication. A different but related strategy can be found in some recent films – of which *Any Given Sunday* is a paradigm – where the simulated sports action is replicated pervasively on television screens within the narrative, with the double motivation of increasing the simulation's sense of realism and acknowledging the degree to which contemporary spectator sport is dominated by media transmission.

(2) The use of archival footage, or location filming, alone, though avoiding the difficulties of simulating sports action, is of limited utility, and generally found (apart from fragmentary scene and subject setting uses) only in the fan film where the protagonists spectate rather than participate, and the sports action, given very sparingly, takes second place to spectatorial reactions off the pitch, in front of the TV or remembering events once witnessed. Various football films provide illustrative instances: (i) Location Shooting: In *Purely Belter* (Mark Herman, 2000) the boys who had expected tickets for a Newcastle United game, unexpectedly find themselves watching at the local enemy Sunderland's stadium, where the game is only background to the comedy of their nervousness; in *Offside* (Jafar Panahi, 2006), the girls, having been apprehended by the authorities, only glimpse fragments of the game played just out of their sight. (ii) Television archival film: in *The Cup* (Kyentse Nhorbu, 2000) and *La Gran Final* (Gerardo Olivares, 2006) the only access the fans have to the game

is TV, which they eventually watch, but the narrative largely consists in their getting to the point of viewing, not in following the game in detail. In *Looking For Eric* (Ken Loach, 2009) the only moments of football action are the brief memories of Cantona's brilliance shown through TV clips as Eric the fan talks with the footballing Eric.

CG and other developments

Chak De India! has a credit for the company 'reelsports solutions' known for work on *Jerry Maguire* (Cameron Crowe, 1996), *Coach Carter* (Thomas Carter, 2005), and other films, who advertise themselves as 'leaders in the field of creating authentic sports action for the screen', based on casting of participants with dual acting and athletic talents and long preproduction coaching in order to bring non-players (aided by camera selection, enhancement and so on) to convincing levels of skill.

Earlier films sometimes used technological sleight of hand to heighten performance realism, perhaps the best (retrospectively) known instance being the invisible 'flipping' of images of the right handed Gary Cooper batting and running so as to match the left handed Lou Gehrig in *Pride of the Yankees*. With the development of CGI, sports special effects, like others, entered a new era. In *Wimbledon*, the film's tennis games are substantially CGI created. Paul Bettany and Kirsten Dunst were trained, not to become adequate players who could be made to look better by careful shooting and editing (like Katharine Hepburn, a games player in real life, playing with Gussie Moran and others in *Pat and Mike*), but to execute shots that looked expert, without hitting the ball, which was then computer-inserted into the scene, creating the artifice-laden hyperrealism typical of CGI effects. In Sori's Japanese film *Ping Pong*, made with similar CGI manipulation, the more extraordinary effects imitate *manga* comic book visuals, with hyperbolic close-ups, e.g. an enormous ball gripping the hugely defined rubber points on the bat before sliding off, and freeze frames of the seemingly gravitation free players smashing in mid-air. It is likely that firms like 'sports solutions' and CG effects will play a growing role in future sports sequences; however, a distinction should be made between films whose *raison d'être* is closely tied to spectacle, and those where the off-field drama may so much outweigh the action sequences that extremes of authentic-seeming simulation are hardly missed (e.g. *Bang the Drum Slowly*, John D.Hancock,

Special effects in
Sori's *Ping Pong*

1973, or *When Billie Beat Bobby,* where in the tennis match very noticeably both players never appear in the same frame).

The fan film

Most sports films centre on players and coaches, but those portraying spectating within the narrative reflect the sports audience's important role. With professional sports, which most films deal with, these watchers are paying customers on whose loyalty the sport and its players depend. Or we may see them in contemporary films watching via television, paying in an oblique, mediated way – the dominant mode of following sports and of sports generating income in the contemporary global media world.

With amateur sports and the films built around them the audiences are usually smaller (if we except the past where sports like tennis, rugby union and athletics were amateur but attracted large attendances, as the still predominantly amateur Gaelic games of hurling and Irish football, and college American football do in the present) – e.g. the local community in American high school basketball and football films like *Hoosiers* (David Anspaugh, 1986), *Remember the Titans*, *Friday Night Lights* (Peter Berg, 2004) and *Coach Carter*, or predominantly friends and family in films about recreational players, e.g. *The Bad News Bears*, *Playing Away*, *Les Boys*, *Up' n'Under*. All these audiences also have a specifically cinematic role comparable to that of the musical's internal audience, of creating the illusion for the external viewer of being present amongst the crowd, a strategy basic to television coverage of actual sports events. Thus any spectator sport film, documentary or fiction, contains passages foregrounding the crowd, with both Riefenstahl and Ichikawa in their Olympic Games documentaries watching the watchers, Riefenstahl most notoriously with shots of Hitler, Goebbels and Göring spectating, but alongside many of other spectators following the action, often with a commitment innocent of politics. In one fleeting but memorable vignette, a woman raptly watches the American shotputter, Sam Francis, throw, and then exuberantly mimics his actions, a reminder of the involvements, identifications and ecstasies audiences gain from sports (effects replicated among the more intimate audiences in films dramatising recreational sports).

Fans, though, are unpredictable, capable of turning against their heroes, as when Lou Gehrig's illness causes his play to decline in *Pride of the Yankees* and fans jeer him as they also rubbish the ageing Babe Ruth in *The Babe Ruth Story*. In his famous farewell speech a forgetful Gehrig idealises their undying loyalty. Gehrig's idealisations tend to typify the sports film's treatment of fans, but there are films where the emotions released by sport are seen more negatively, an extreme instance, discussed below, being *The Fan* (1996).

In certain films constituting the subtype the fan film, the fan within the narrative moves to the centre, either as single or group protagonist, of films as different as the psychological thriller of malign over-identification, *The Fan*; various British football hooligan fictions and documentaries (e.g. *The Firm*, Alan Clarke, 1988), equally at the pathological end of the scale; the romantic comedy, *Fever Pitch* (David Evans, 1997); Ken Loach's benign

Watchers watched in
Riefenstahl's *Olympia*

Looking For Eric; child-centred comedies, e.g. *P'tang Yang Kipperbang* (Michael Apted, 1982), *Wondrous Oblivion* (Paul Morrison, 2003), *Purely Belter* (Mark Herman, 2000) and *Breaking Away* (Peter Yates, 1980); narratives, or parts of narratives, the inverse of the hooligan films, following travelling fans, e.g. *Allez France!* (Robert Dhéry and Pierre Tchernia, 1964) about French rugby enthusiasts in London for an international, or in memorable miniature the famous comedy of Charters and Caldicott, bluff cricket followers caught up in the comedy-thrillers Hitchcock's *The Lady Vanishes* (1938) and Carol Reed's *Night Train to Munich* (1940); and, lastly a subgroup of recent films about fans' efforts to access games or broadcasts from which they are excluded, including *Purely Belter* again, *The Cup* (Khyentse Norbu, 1999), *La Gran Final* (Gerardo Olivares, 2006), and the Iranian film *Offside* (Jafar Panahi, 2006), in which girls prohibited by religio-sexual regulations from attending a World Cup football qualifier in Tehran attempt to gain entry. Finally, that apotheosis of the fan film, *Field of Dreams* is discussed in chapter 3.

The fan identifies with the team or certain players (or sometimes more broadly with the game), an identification which may be life-enhancing as when Ken Loach, *apropos* of his film *Looking For Eric* asserts 'It's a prop that sustains us when the rest of one's life is in tatters. Following a player or team can sustain you through the imagination' (Stern 2009: 98). *The Fan*, however, plays balefully on the term fan's origin in the word fanatic. Here Robert De Niro, with overtones of his celebrity-obsessed Rupert Pupkin in Scorsese's *The King of Comedy* (1982), places on the baseball player Bobby Rayburn bought by his team for $40 million too many of the hopes of a fast disintegrating life. At the film's beginning he recites a poem he has written, containing many sentiments the ordinary fan might feel, *'excited and anxious I await my dream/Opening day I can always trust/... the return of our hero does brighten the days/Just briefly my troubles get lost in the haze...'*. Even the more negative feelings he articulates are hardly in themselves abnormal, a critique with which better balanced observers might feel some empathy – *'The players say now they play for themselves/ This causes a burning within me that dwells/The fan is the one that pays for the game/That bestows all the riches and welcome fame/The players listen but really don't hear...'*. But as his life disintegrates, Gil becomes increasingly hung up on Rayburn's contemporary athlete's commodification of self and sport and increasingly unbalanced in over-personalising his relationship with the performer, eventually invading Rayburn's off-field life with fatal results.

The child as fan, the fan as child

The child is the absolute fan's prototype, approaching the sport and the sports star unconditionally, granting the game and its players an unqualified heroic status uncomplicated by life's complexities. Two English cricket films, *Wondrous Oblivion* and *P'tang Yang Kipperbang* have boy protagonists enwrapped in dreams of the sport. In both, though, the child's innocent obsession is compromised by contingent realities, in the latter linked to the protagonist's eventual disillusion with other fantasies, of romantic love in his ethereal passion for a girl, and dreams of World War II heroism placed on the young school groundsman eventually arrested for desertion. Similarly, in *Wondrous Oblivion*, the neighbourhood's prejudice against the West Indian family whom the young Jewish protagonist, David Wiseman, befriends through cricket, his betrayal of their daughter because of peer pressures, and the looming responsibilities of Jewish manhood as his parents decide to move to a better area, precipitate his taking leave of his earlier life in which he hands his collection of cricket cards, which come to life to bid farewell to him, to the West Indian daughter. Both films' farewells are presumably not to all interest in the beloved sport (by the close of *Wondrous Oblivion*, the protagonist's Central European father, reconnecting with his son, is learning the game), but to the child's naïve view of it as a wholly self-contained world. Though the romantic football comedy *Fever Pitch* has an adult protagonist, he might be seen as a man-child coming to his leavetaking of a too-consuming commitment, under the influence of his girlfriend's pregnancy, and the fulfilment of his dreams of Arsenal winning the League: 'My relationship with Arsenal changed that night. It was as if I'd jumped onto the shoulders of the team and they carried me into the light that suddenly shone down on all of us. And the lift they gave me enabled me to part company with them in some ways. We still see each other all the time and I still love and hate them all at the same time. But I have my own life now. My own successes and failures aren't necessarily mixed up with theirs. And that's got to be a good thing, I suppose.'

That 'I suppose' suggests a melancholy attached to the loss of the child's vision of the game in all three films, and justifies the comic approval that might be given to the end of *Breaking Away*. There the late adolescent protagonist (far better at his sport than any of the above), having been cured of his attempts to metamorphose himself into an Italian through over-identification with his racing cyclist heroes, by their brutally fouling him when he challenges them in a race, proves incorrigible when his meeting with a French girl is clearly about to send him via fantasies of the Tour de France into turning himself into a Frenchman, these European dreams an escape from his restricted Indiana environment.

Four football films (*Purely Belter*, *Offside*, *The Cup* and *La Gran Final*, from Britain, Iran, Bhutan/Australia, and Spain, respectively), comprise a subgroup built around fans' attempts to view events (either live – *Purely Belter* and *Offside*, or on TV – *The Cup* and *La Gran Final*) from which they are excluded. The reasons for exclusion differ substantially. In *Purely Belter* the boys undertake scams to fund expensive Newcastle United season tickets, a dream combining a passion for football with momentary entry to a socio-economic class far from their deprived circumstances, as well as memories or fantasies of father/son bondings through football. In *Offside* the Tehran girls, whose passion for football equals that of the males, resist bans on their attendance at a big game, some of the most incisive sequences being where they interact with the young soldiers guarding them when apprehended, male/female interchanges which subvert the authorities' attempts at sexual segregation, and also suggest the harm such segregation does, to males as well as females. The 'exotic' audiences in *The Cup* and *La Gran Final* trying to see the 1992 or 1996 football World Cup finals on television are situated in Bhutan, Mongolia, Niger and the Amazon rainforest, testifying to football's global popularity. *La Gran Final*'s epigraph provides a moral, which is only one of many meanings played out in the film, but by its prominence invites contemplation, i.e. the difficulty these third world fans have in viewing the game compared with its ease of access in the developed world. In *The Cup* the exiled Tibetan boys in a Bhutanese Buddhist monastery persuade the elders to let them hire a television to watch the final, an act which has poignant moral consequences for one of them. This subtle film creates a rare comedy of perspectives on sport when the more worldly assistant abbot answers the elderly abbot's questions about the World Cup: 'Two civilized nations fighting over a ball'/'You must be joking. So there's violence?'/ 'Sometimes'/ 'How about sex?'/ 'Don't worry. There's no sex.'

The comic of sport

The great theorists of the comic, Freud (*Jokes and Their Relation to the Unconscious*) and Bergson (*Laughter*), initiate their discussions with simple physical examples that read like descriptions of the earliest silent film gags. Bergson's 'basal' instance of comedy is an inattentive running man tripping on an unseen obstacle; while Freud's funny walker demonstrates comparison as the motor of the comic – think of *College* (James W. Horne, 1927) where athletes sprint, throw, hurdle, jump and vault perfectly, preluding Buster Keaton's comic débacles, e.g. the shot's unexpected weight overbalancing him onto his back. Both theorists anchor their arguments corporeally before moving to the diffused complexities of verbal comedy, a gradation suggesting film's historical movement from silence to sound. However, the opposition physical = simple: verbal = complex is untenable, since the great comedians' physical registers are multifariously and subtly expressive. While sound comedy often features wordless comic action, and silent comedy sometimes foregrounds verbal wit through intertitles, nevertheless the most extended deployment of the comic possibilities of the body in motion is found in silent comedy, with Keaton in particular recalling, both seriously and comically, Eadweard Muybridge's celebrated stop motion photographic studies of athletes in *Animal Locomotion* (1887) and *The Human Figure in Motion* (1901).

Seven topoi dominate the comedy of the games-playing body, though often in complicating combinations. (1) *Comedy of Fear* – directly physical in the boxing film, or other contact sports (as when Lloyd in *The Freshman*, Harold Lloyd, 1925, mistakes the detached leg of the tackling dummy for his own) but fear of hurt may extend to fear of less directly physical failure or exposure. (2) *Comedy of Incompetence* – as in the examples from *College*, the most prolific category since the techniques of sports are difficult to master yet easy to stand in judgement over. (3) *Comedy of Over Confidence* with its pride before fall trajectory. (4) *Comedy of Bodily Address*, often directly linked to (3), based on exaggeration of stance, preparatory gestures and so on and usually followed quickly by abject exposure. (5) *Comedy of Infracted Rules* where a comic figure, through ignorance or design, flagrantly breaks the conventions of a sport's intensely rule-governed activities. This, unlike 1–4 above, may tend as much to success as failure, with success always the case with (6) *Comedy of Reversal* in which the previously hopeless protagonist defies all but generic expectations to triumph, and (7) *Comedy of Supercompetence,* most often linked to (6) where the comic figure's unexpected mastery is so exaggerated as to be ludicrous.

To amplify. (1) *Fear.* Keaton in *Battling Butler* (Keaton, 1926), impersonating a boxer, when hit, turns away and slaps ineffectually, face averted, 'like a girl' (pre-*Million Dollar Baby*). In *City Lights* (Chaplin, 1931) Chaplin, diminutive, pale, unmuscled, also finds himself boxing. Pre-fight, he lights his vicious opponent's cigarette appeasingly, making excessively feminised gestures suggesting sexual dimorphism and submission, signs so flirtatiously feminised that the opponent interprets them as homosexual overtures, pointedly undressing out of his view. As proponent of the most violent sport, the boxer may be imagined the most masculine and heterosexual of men – certainly by Mae West's muscle-loving heroines – but the sport's intense homosociality may also suggest homosexual themes as in Carné's *L'Air de Paris* and Scorsese's *Raging Bull*. Fighting, Chaplin's tramp moves in balletic synchronisation with the referee, placing the official constantly between himself and his opponent, giving himself an unfairly protected position from which to attack.

(2) *Incompetence.* Both Chaplin and Keaton in the sequences above demonstrate memorable incapacity. The tramp even puts his boxing gloves on the wrong hands. Both have extreme difficulty even entering the ring, getting trapped in the ropes in elaborately different ways. In *The Freshman* Harold Lloyd (still wearing his trademark glasses as Chaplin still wears his hat in the dressing room) is given a football to punt. A figure retreats to receive this aerial bombardment. Harold waves him further back. He kicks and the ball sails backward over his head. In these first two categories motifs of emasculation and effeminisation are common, depending on the standards of masculinity the sportsman supposedly embodies and the female's perceived incapacity for muscular action, though with the cultural change of widespread female sports participation, this last is becoming less common. The moment in *His Girl Friday* (Howard Hawks, 1940) when Hildy (Rosalind Russell) perfectly tackles a fleeing male, while exemplifying her extraordinariness and difference from the average female, and complicatedly part of Hawks' conception of the man's woman, may in the age of the first American female sports stars, cinematically mark an important acceleration of these changes.

(3) *Overconfidence*, (4) *Bodily Address*. Overconfidence may orginate either in naïve ignorance, or in overbearing self-deception, with the latter because of its psychological complexities the most fruitfully comic. Lloyd in *The Freshman* enacts the former, W.C.Fields in his early sound film *The Golf Specialist* (Monte Brice, 1930), the latter as he plays golf to impress a sexually available young woman. Golf, identified with masculine mastery, is here clearly an instrument of seduction, with Fields suggestively announcing the performance of an explosive tee shot. In fact, though the sketch lasts twenty minutes, the shot is never played, delayed and interrupted as it is by his ludicrous monologues, his defective caddy's incompetences, by Fieldsian comedy of frustration (hat dislodging as he addresses the ball, a pie getting attached to his shoe), and by his repeated exaggerated flexing and elaborate readdressing of the ball after each interruption. The non-consummation of the explosive shot suggests the unlikeliness of any sexual outcome, even if he had escaped the arrest that terminates the sketch, the protagonist's sexual abilities being as doubtful as his golf skills, all approach and no follow through. The comedy of address works best with games like golf, cricket and baseball or serving in tennis and related games where the batter or hitter has a relatively long predominantly static foreplay period of waiting during which signs of (fake) expertise may abound.

(5) *Infracted Rules and Conventions*. Comedy may derive from a sport's rules and conventions being broken in ignorance due to the player's naïvete. More extraordinary are subversions that are either knowing or instinctive, as most memorably with the Marx brothers in *Horse Feathers* (Norman Z. McLeod, 1932). In the American football game between Huxley and Darwin, Groucho, Huxley's principal, Professor Wagstaffe, undermines the game's rules by dashing onto the field in academic gown to down an opposing player. No one objects, the game's laws apparently suspended by the force of his subversion. The serious business of football signals (learnt and guarded with military zeal) are parodied by Chico in sound passages: 'Uno, duo, tre, vendi,/Thisa time we go left endi.' Midgame, the brothers play cards on the field, Groucho briefly rejoins the spectators to get a woman's phone number, Harpo, in his muteness the epitome of silent comedy in the sound era, sits on the ball and eats a banana, using the skins to down opposing players, and then, as municipal dogcatcher, temporarily abandons the game to chase a dog straying onto the pitch. Finally, mounting a horse-drawn cart, he drives to the Darwin goal line where he unloads

Groucho subverts
the sporting ethos
in *Horse Feathers*

ball after ball for multiple touchdowns, which, though plainly illegal, win a game made as lawless by the brothers' hedonistic subversions of sport's disciplines, as is their triple marriage with the 'college widow' at the film's end.

(6) *Reversal.* The least interesting of the topoi largely relying on generic motivations, pleasure at a happy ending, and revelation of the hero's hidden skills coinciding with the sports film's conventional last minute victory, despite the preceding narrative having made it highly unlikely. At *The Freshman*'s football game climax, the incompetent Harold runs in an amazing touchdown, just as in *Battling Butler* Keaton defeats the real boxer ouside the ring in an equally amazing display of fighting. For both, the love of a girl is the catalyst, as is also the case at the end of *College* which, though equally implausible, has the formal satisfactions of the many activities at which the hero failed in his early attempts to win the girl (sprinting, hurdling, various throwings, jumping, vaulting, pitching, batting) being successfully recapitulated as he rescues her. Though with Keaton such switcharounds have a kind of motivation in the star's obvious athleticism even as he fails, Chaplin's commitment to pathos means that he avoids such wish-fulfilling outcomes, his fight in *City Lights* ending with him unconscious.

(7) *Supercompetence.* In *Pool Sharks* (Edwin Middleton, 1915) W. C. Fields and his rival for a young woman play pool. The narrative combines both mens' incompetence in most matters, particularly in courting the girl, with improbable super-competence in the game. Both are so almost super-

naturally skilled that trick photography is needed with shots of the balls doing impossible things, i.e. all disappearing into the pockets then emerging again to reassemble into the beginning of game cluster. This is too good to be true, and pool is forgotten as game-playing regresses to warfare, using cue, sticks and balls as weapons.

The many kinds of verbal comedy generated by sports are too various to be categorised, from Abbott and Costello's 'Who's on first?' baseball routine in *A Night in the Tropics* (A. Edward Sutherland,1940); to 'You Knock Me Out' in *It's Always Fair Weather* (Stanley Donen and Gene Kelly, 1955) where Cyd Charisse enchants Stillman's Gym by reciting the heavyweight champions from Sullivan to Marciano, to the sophisticated wit centred around cricket, public school and Oxbridge affiliations in Hitchcock's *The Lady Vanishes* and Reed's *Night Train to Munich*. Nevertheless, body-oriented gags dominate sports comedy even in the sound era. Thus in Harold Lloyd's *The Milky Way*, where an unathletic milkman is mistaken for a boxer, Lloyd is as inventively physical as earlier, e.g. varying the homosocial/homosexual motif as he surreptitiously searches for his lost lucky charm down the back of his opponent's shorts, or where, sight obscured in a clinch, his attempts to punch his opponent deliver blows to his own elbow, which in turn propels involuntary uppercuts to his own chin. In the remake, *The Kid From Brooklyn* (Norman Z. McLeod, 1946) with Danny Kaye, the sporting comedy is significantly almost wholly derived from Lloyd's predominantly non-verbal routines.

The female sports film

While entertainment films are never dominated by radical arguments, they characteristically respond to emerging trends (as witness the female boxing film, that extreme representative of women's entry into previously exclusively male sports), if not in their most unsettling form. As if to contradict this, the otherwise unconventional Spanish film *La Gran Final*, its narrative spanning three third world countries, presents moments in which women in Mongolia, Niger and Amazonian Brazil, express impatience with the men's desire to watch the football World Cup final on television – suggesting that women (whether because of different priorities – 'the soaps' are more attractive in two of the cases – or because sports have been closed to them) are less interested in sport than men. This comic clash of interests derives from a longstanding consensus on differing male and female attitudes that it might be premature to dismiss unconditionally, but which certainly can no longer be seen as unquestionably fixed, especially in leisure-abundant first world societies.

In older sports films, women act not as athletes but as supporters of male athletes, like, typically, Lou Gehrig's mother and wife in *The Pride of the Yankees*. However, other representations beyond the sports film, suggest shifting realities e.g. Hildy's pursuit of Warden Cooley in *His Girl Friday*, hiking up her skirt to run, then launching her perfect tackle and laying low ideas of female physical incapacity. Similar implications are enacted by dynamic female dancers (e.g. Cyd Charisse, Ann Miller, Eleanor Powell) in the 1940s/1950s musical, whose strenuous physicality equally interrogates ideologies of feminine frailty, as does the aquatic athleticism of Esther Williams, a national swimming champion before becoming a film star. Charisse's 'Baby, you knock me out' in *It's Always Fair Weather* fuses athletic performance with verbal and visual boxing tropes, including her recital of the heavyweight champions.

In *Pat and Mike*, Katharine Hepburn plays a prodigious athlete and Spencer Tracy her manager, a very different situation from *Woman of the Year* (George Stevens, 1942) where her feminist polymath disdains Tracy's occupation as sports reporter. Though implicated in criminality, Mike encourages Pat's sporting genius, partly for financial gain, but also more disinterestedly. Whereas her younger fiancé has a version of the 'male gaze', less erotic than ultracritical, which renders her helpless when watched by him – as in the expressionist tennis scene where, playing 'Gorgeous

Cyd Charisse in *It's Always Fair Weather*

Gussie' Moran on the professional circuit, Moran's racquet grows huge and Hepburn's shrinks – Mike's gaze is benevolent. This female athlete and male coach/manager coupling reflected an uncontested status quo, but the film, by making Mike shed his criminality and revise his patriarchial position, does more than uncritically sustain it, though along the way Pat's physical strength provokes a version of the Tracy character's difficulties with woman as 'competitor' common to their romantic comedy encounters.

The female athlete/male coach dyad becomes a continuing convention of the female sports film. This may be variously interpreted. (i) As regressively keeping the woman under patriarchal domination. (ii) As accurately reflecting real world conditions, despite female advances, of male sporting dominance and female dependence. (iii) Given that most popular films feature both a leading male and female, in films centred on women athletes the coach/manager is an obvious leading male role, with interesting possibilities for friction and female assertion, as in *Personal Best* where Tingloff never wholly controls, professionally and sexually, his female charges Chris and Tory. (iv) Since most female sports films have heroines overcoming prejudice and convincing sceptics, usually male, of their abilities, the coach/manager plays a pivotal role as the expert, as distinct from uninterested or hostile males (like the spectator burlesquing the girls in *A League of Their Own*, weeping because he has supposedly broken a nail!), whose eventual conversion is doubly meaningful. A prime instance is Joey Dugan (Tom Hanks) in *A League of Their Own*, converted from initial disgust with coaching women ('There's no crying in baseball!') who finally chooses to stay with the women's game rather than coaching men. Jesminder's coach in *Bend It Like Beckham,* though always committed to his women's team, makes a similar decision. In *Gracie* (Davis Guggenheim, 2007) the heroine's football coach father is converted to coaching her, as is the school team coach into playing her in the boys' team.

Most female sports films begin with female sport demeaningly secondarised, generating narratives in which the protagonists grapple with an obstacle largely peculiar to the sportswoman. In *Chak De India!* the national hockey board's attitudes are shockingly revealed – 'Indian women are born to cook and clean; they cannot run around in short skirts'. Where Indian men's hockey has declined in success and popularity in the face of the commercial power of cricket, women's hockey struggles for any recognition at all, but after many vicissitudes the team win the world championship, vindicating the Indian women's game and female sport generally. In *A League of Their Own* (Penny Marshall, 1992), based on the actual mid-western women's baseball league (1943–54), professional women's baseball is instituted only because of the wartime draft. Like many fictions based on historical events, the film alters fact for dramatic purposes, boosting the girls league's importance by erroneously suggesting that the war terminated men's baseball, and then obscuring the women's game's close relation to softball. While an important narrative emphasis is the girls winning over sceptical audiences, another is their experiencing female solidarities and freedoms released by wartime disruptions (the supportive Ira Lowenstein compares the players threatened with post-war redundancy to 'Rosie the Riveter' about to be pushed off the production line). However constricting the league's deportment lessons and sexually titillating outfits are – and however much they cast the players as voyeuristic experience for the male audience (grotesquely parodied by the dressing room peeping of the male child, Stillwell) – the league offers its wartime escapees freedom from conformity. This is something the film's focal figure, Dottie Hinson (Geena Davis), always something of an outsider in the group, happily married, only staying briefly until her husband's discharge, and initially reluctant to attend the reunion forty years on, comes to understand. Conversing privately, one of the girls explains staying with her abusive partner, because he was the only man available for a girl who, liking sport, was treated as 'weird' and 'strange', even 'not like a girl', but goes on to say that since joining the league she has found many others like her. At which she tears up his photograph. The sequence can be read doubly, as referring to heterosexual girls whose only 'strangeness' is playing sports, or as covertly alluding to the sexual difference which *A League of Their Own*, like other women's sports films – *Personal Best* being the exception – is reluctant to dramatise openly, a reluctance even more evident in male sports films (where the pleasant comedy in *Les Boys* based around the ice hockey playing lawyer's homosexuality and the rest of the team's reaction to it is exceptional). Where spoken, as in *Bend It Like Beckham* and *Gracie*, it tends to be raised and simultaneously denied – in Gracie's girlfriend warning her that neglecting her social life for soccer may lead to her being branded a 'lesbo', and in *Bend It Like Beckham* in Jools' mother's comic fretting about locker room lesbianism leading her to misinterpret the girls' quarrel over their male coach as a same-sex lovers' dispute. 'Compulsory heterosexuality' in the presentation of both real and screen world women's sports (as well as men's) is influenced by conservative pressures from sponsoring organisations and sports bodies, by attritional male attitudes, but also in female sports by heterosexual sportswomen's understandable desire not to present their sports as lesbian-dominated (*Gracie*'s epilogue title claims that post Title IX, 5 million girls play soccer in the US). Hence *When Billie Beat Bobby*, though made in 1991 well after Billie Jean King's coming out, makes no reference to it. The only female sports films which dramatise sexuality between women are *Dawn!* and *Personal Best* where the rival pentathletes Chris and Tory have a relationship with openly sexual scenes. Their relationship does not survive their track rivalry and the more heterosexual element of Chris's bisexuality pushes her predictably towards a male partner, but it is presented in uncensorious terms as part of the film's interest in the bisexual erotics of the athletic body.

The tennis melodrama *Hard Fast and Beautiful* (Ida Lupino, 1951), falls outside the female sports film's affirmative template. Rather than forming its 1940s/1950s 'woman's film' narrative around the accomplishments of its young female tennis player, it focuses on a negative version of the mother daughter bond (cf. Charlotte and her dictatorial mother in *Now Voyager,* Irving Rapper, 1942), with Claire Trevor attempting to live through her daughter's talents, only to drive her from the game into domesticity. The mother's role, malign here, but usually background and supporting a male athlete, is reworked in two recent American teen girl 'soccer' films, *Gracie* and *Soccer Mom* (Gregory McClatchy, 2008). Although the daughter in the girl surfing film *Blue Crush* suffers from her promiscuous mother's absence, in the 'soccer' films the mothers encourage their daughter's ambitions in the traditional manner, but supporting a daughter rather than a son.

In its various forms, the female sports film, characterised by struggle and success, is a gendered version of the traditional affirmative sports film. The sports history film *When Billie Beat Bobby* and the biopic *Heart Like A Wheel* offer variations on this pattern. The former, beginning with an assertive feminist celebration of Billie Jean King, has a finale of hyperbolical reactions to her victory – a cascade of statements by women inspired by it to pursue success in other fields. Yet the narrative tends to subvert the film's main event, presenting the tennis challenge as a piece of hustling by the

55 year-old Riggs, decades past serious tennis, unfit and too commercially preoccupied to practice properly, the creation of media hype, incapable of bearing the meanings imposed on it. *Heart like a Wheel*, the biopic of the drag racer Shirley Muldowney, less didactic and less riven by contradiction, follows a pattern close to the female country singer biopic, of struggle in a male-dominated business, single motherhood, abusive relationships, failed marriage, unsuccessful extra-marital relationship, but ultimate professional success. The broken relationships are in no way presented as of the heroine's making, except perhaps through mistaken choice of men, and seem, rather than a punishment for overreaching, the product of the peripatetic nature of the sporting career, and male difficulties in accepting the woman's professionally equal or dominant role.

The race-centred sports film

Two contemporary films situated before segregated baseball ended just after World War Two, and thus focused wholly on white players, *8 Men Out* (set in 1919) and *A League of Their Own* (in 1943), briefly but incisively acknowledge American sport's history of racial injustice. In the latter, a ball is picked up on the peripheries by a young black woman who hurls it back to Dottie Hinson. Surprised by her perfect throw, Dottie nods appreciatively, while the thrower's meaningful look makes an unspoken point about the league's opportunities for women being for whites only. In the former, Ring Lardner and a colleague chat with Winslow, a black man whose menial job is clearing stadium rubbish. Winslow, asked about the 1919 White Sox, says they are 'the best we seen yet', adding, 'best white folks team anyway', a reminder of the black players barred from white baseball by unwritten gentlemen's agreements. Both moments allude to the segregated past from the vantage point of integrated American sports, an integration now so pronounced that *Sports Movie*'s burlesque has an affluent white boy, George Johnson, seek greater street cred by assuming a Latino persona ('It's pronounced Jorge Juanson') forty years on from Mailer's 'white negro' hipster in 'The White Negro: Superficial Reflections on the Hipster' (1957) – a switch reflecting the rise in Hispanic American baseball players. Major league baseball's two fifths Hispanic-Americans, Afro-Americans and Asians, and basketball's and American football's 70–80% black players have been seen as prompting a Hollywood cycle nostalgic for white centrality. In that retrospective 1950s basketball drama *Hoosiers* (David Anspaugh, 1986), before the white rural Indiana high school team defeats the black-dominated city team, the ritual pre-game prayer alludes to David and Goliath, with the whites rather than the blacks seen as biblical underdogs, despite their social advantages (a case where sport's sphere of opportunity for the marginalised is clear, yet also its deceptiveness as regards the larger society). The Afro-American predominance in American football and, particularly, basketball, is thus less positive than it may superficially seem with celebrity black athletes' wealth not only vastly untypical, but obscuring the way in which for many the lure of unlikely sporting stardom blocks off other ambition, and also perpetuates purely physical stereotypes of Afro-Americanness.

Made in the early 1950s rather than reminiscing about them, the first mainstream American sports films with black protagonists, the biopics *The Jackie Robinson Story* and *The Joe Louis Story* were cut-price productions because of their subject matter, undesirability for the South, and lack of star actors – in contrast to the triumvirate in the later comedy based around the pre-war negro baseball leagues, *The Bingo Long Travelling All Stars and Motor Kings* (John Badham, 1976) with James Earl Jones, Billy Dee Williams and Richard Pryor, and Will Smith in *Ali* and Wesley Snipes in *White Men Can't Jump* (Ron Shelton, 1992).

These breakthrough biopics provide easy pickings for ideological deconstruction. Their studied avoidance – despite some strong dramatisations of colour prejudice in the Robinson film – of showing the racism dramatised as endemic, their paternalistic narration (the white reporter mourning the aged Louis's defeat by Marciano before celebrating his greatness, the representative conservative-liberal white framing voice extolling Robinson), and their insistence on stoical patience as the way forward for Afro-Americans, are plain to see. But the compromises imposed by their historical moment need to be understood as the condition of their existence, for instance the presentation of Joe Louis onscreen, no less than offscreen, as the antithesis of the only previous black heavyweight champion, Jack Johnson, driven into exile for his refusal to act the subservient negro, especially in flaunting sexual relations with white women. Nevertheless, the heart of the film is Joe's relationship with his black trainer, 'Chappie' Blackburn, who, rather than any white man, disciplines the boxer's talents, contradicting the view that the black sportsman only attains discipline through white overseeing.

In *The Jackie Robinson Story*, Robinson's chief mentor is white, the Dodgers' manager, Branch Rickey, who persuades him to meet prejudice with forbearance. Nevertheless, Rickey's transcending of racism is not presented as unalloyedly principled, but a convenient fusion of egalitarianism with capitalist acumen, for, searching for profits, he has been talent hunting in Latin America before experimenting with a black player. At the film's end, Robinson, testifying to The House Committee on Unamerican Activities, is drafted as a Cold War warrior, an anti-Paul Robeson (who for his radical critiques of American racism and his relations with the USSR had his passport withdrawn in the 1950s) as well as an anti-Johnson, proving America the land of democratic opportunity for all races, though with a concession to reality in his admission that his case is exceptional. As he finishes, the Statue of Liberty is superimposed on his image, a trope continued as the ending repeats the opening image of Robinson as a child walking along a road, back to camera so that his colour is hidden, while the voice over insists on the Americanness of its story –in one sense a rhetoric optimistic in its inclusiveness but at the same time heavily tendentious in its too easy disposal of the specifics of Afro-American disadvantage.

By the time of *The Great White Hope* in 1970, Johnson could be portrayed as a hero, his victimisation compared with Muhammed Ali's Vietnam draft persecution, and his provocative sexuality seen as a harbinger of relaxing interracial attitudes, though a scene where a black activist condemns Johnson for his dealings with whites parallels Elijah Muhammed's condemnation of Ali's, recognising new inflections of racial division. Twenty years later in *White Men Can't Jump* the focus switches to a comedy of white-black interchanges less one directional than the rules of behaviour imposed on the biopics' black heroes, or on Ali by both whites and blacks, or Mailer's white hipsters' raids on black style, a give and take between white and black orientations by the basketball court con artists played by Wesley Snipes and Woody Harrelson.

The American sports film's dealings with race have both historical and quantitative precedence, but the thematic of sport as the preeminent field where the racially marginalised may compete with or even defeat the dominant, is played out in the cinemas of other nations in ways at one level cross-culturally similar, but at another marked by the difference of unique situations belonging to unique places, as in two films, one Australian, *Australian Rules*, the other English, *Playing Away*.

Australian Rules

The title *Australian Rules* plays on the double meaning Australian Rules Football and the rules (official and unofficial) of Australian society. The film is set in a small South Australian fishing town, hence the breeding and selling of maggots which provides a metaphor for the realities beneath its 'tidy town' image. In this regressive space largely untouched by any changing attitudes to the indigenous population, whites and aborigines basically interact in only three ways: sexually – through white males' casual use of aboriginal girls; criminally – through crimes committed on white property by aboriginal youths; and, more hopefully, through sport – with the town's successful football team half made up of aborigines. Transgressing the boundaries erected between the game and wider social life, the friendship between a white boy, Gary Black (Blacky), the film's focal character, and his aboriginal mate, Dumby Red, is central, their bonding through football and callow sexual fantasies of the white Australian stars Nicole Kidman and Kylie Minogue, deepened by their both seeking an escape route from the blighted town – Dumby through his Australian Rules prowess which has already attracted big city interest, Blacky through his naïve attempts at self-education. The context of Dumby's possible escape is double: on the one hand, the blighting of aboriginal life by Australia's former authoritarian control of the indigenous population, its malign consequences persisting in alcoholism, poverty, unemployment, crime and early mortality; on the other hand, aboriginal achievement in various sports, particularly boxing, rugby and, above all, Australian Rules where up to 10% of the Australian Football League's players are of aboriginal descent, success stories very different from the tragic trajectories in the 1900s and 1930s of the fast bowlers Jack Marsh and Eddie Gilbert.

But the success on national and international stages of football stars, Lionel Rose (boxing), Yvonne Goolagong (tennis), Cathy Freeman (athletics), and others, hardly touches the bleak realities of life in *Australian Rules*. The film's catastrophe follows the team's winning of the local final, when Dumby is denied the 'best on field' award, which goes to the white coach's son, a '*goonya*' (white) injustice which angers Dumby into a symbolically reciprocal burglary, in which he is shot dead by Blacky's father, pushing Blacky into open positions of paternal and social opposition (attending Dumby's funeral and beginning a serious relationship with Dumby's sister,

Clarence). At the film's end Blacky and Clarence have left the town together, and Blacky's voice over relates the disintegration of the football team after the aborigines withdraw from it.

Playing Away

Playing Away, a British film of complex mixed descent (its screenwriter, Caryl Phillips, and its director Horace Ové, both of Caribbean origin) as well as effects, follows a West Indian social cricket team's visit to the wholly white Middle England village of Sneddington, to play the local side as part of the village's 'Third World Week'. The resulting, predominantly comic interactions are generated by sport's double-edged provision of a utopian space in which otherwise socially divided races, ethnicities, religions and classes meet through the hold particular games have over disparate communities, a space, where, to quote the Australian poet, Les Murray's poem 'The Aboriginal Cricketer', 'all the missiles are just leather/and come from one direction' (Murray 2003) – a space, however, potentially fraught with prejudice and payback, depending on the historically and socially conditioned psychologies of the players. As a game that accompanied British imperial expansion, cricket was adopted by various colonised peoples, and became a site of nationalist assertion in the test matches later played between the colonies/post-colonial states and their rulers/ex-rulers, with victory or defeat (as with rugby in some white settler colonies) having great

Comedy of racial difference in *Playing Away*

73

symbolic meaning. *Playing Away,* made during the West Indies' dominance (which has now declined) of international cricket in the late twentieth century, is built around a low level 'friendly' which is, however, as heavily freighted with past and present tensions as any test match, in particular the disappointments of the post-1947 West Indian British diaspora, with its extension of the second classness of the old colonial subjects into a new environment. The seemingly idyllic English village and its cricket field, much celebrated from Dingley Dell versus All-Muggleton in Dickens' *The Pickwick Papers* on (though that narrative includes Mr Jingle's single wicket match with Sir Thomas Blazo in the West Indies, and the death of the exhausted native bowler Quanko Samba), becomes, in spite of the accepted greatness of West Indian players, a scene revealing the forces of prejudice and reactive counter prejudice – most obviously the village bully Fredrick's racist jokes, the rural youths' stalled plan to rape Willie-Boy's daughter, the pub barman refusing to serve Willie-Boy, and the visitors' regressive reactions.

Like the title *Australian Rules*, *Playing Away* has multiple meanings. Visiting rural England, the Brixton West Indians are playing away. Sneddington, though literally at home, are also on unfamiliar ground, playing away, as it were, against opponents they would normally never encounter. In a sense too, for the West Indians, every match is played away – from their pre-diaspora first home, at least for the older ones such as the captain Willie-Boy (Norman Beaton) and his friend, Boots, old enough to be at the tail end of the original SS Empire Windrush Caribbean immigration of the late 1940s and early 1950s, torn between staying and returning, a tension largely foreign to the younger players, whose home is the London Caribbean community. In the film's most subtle workings, both communities are revealed as fractured, with the West Indians further split between those happy to play against whites and those, with their own racist agenda, who are not, by geography – coming as they do from different territories – and by class (Jeff the race relations worker who has jilted one of the girls with the team to marry a middle class white woman). The villagers are profoundly riven by major socio-economic and accompanying cultural differences, most obviously between the well-meaning but naïve Third World Week organisers and the unreconstructed Fredrick and rural underclass youths, though two of the village girls, impelled by the most basic motivations cutting across ideologies, pursue two of the younger West Indians sexually. The game eventually ends farcically when, protesting at umpiring decisions favouring the West

Indians, the underclass section of the Sneddington team walk off, display-ing the lack of sporting values the West Indians are suspected of, mean-ing an easy victory for the 'Brixton Conquisatadors' against the remnants of Sneddington. In the last verbal exchange of the film, when Willie-Boy complains to his team mates about not being offered a post-match drink, his colleague says, 'These people have difficulties of their own', drawing Willie-Boy's sardonic reply, 'You don't think we have ours?', a final underlin-ing of the film's interest not in simply laying blame, but exploring through comedy the intricacies of the situation. Though Geoffrey (Robert Urquhart) the husband of Margery, the force behind the festival, whose umpiring deci-sion sparks the walk off, has lived the British colonial life in Africa for many years, and even visited the Caribbean, it is illustrative of the film's interest in going beyond the stereotypes that certain of the characters, both white and black, at times fall into, that he seems to be the one character in the film who, if from a privileged socio-economic position not open to the West Indians, and perhaps from homosexual interests in young black men, has gathered ironic wisdom from his personal diasporic experiences.

3   FOUR MAJOR SPORTS FILMS

The four films discussed below in more detail than is possible elsewhere embrace both the Hollywood and non-Hollywood cinemas and a range of sports. Two (*Chariots of Fire, Field of Dreams*) exemplify the genre's dominant classical paradigms, while the non-western third (*Lagaan*), exhibits the hybridity of popular Indian cinema, and the fourth (*Any Given Sunday*) utilises a contemporary Hollywood post-classical style. Though the films as individual works show many differences, as generic relatives they also share overlapping concerns and structures. Three of the four (*Chariots of Fire, Lagaan, Any Given Sunday* – the last in a slightly qualified form) employ the traditional victory plot, thus refuting the notion that achievement in the genre demands subversion – as distinct from meaningful development – of that most basic formula. Three (*Chariots of Fire, Any Given Sunday, Field of Dreams*) invoke nostalgia for a better past, a persistent generic trait registering ambivalences at the heart of highly commodified modern sport. All four employ sport as a synecdoche of larger social (*Any Given Sunday*), national (*Lagaan, Chariots of Fire*), even metaphysical thematics (*Field of Dreams*), and contradict the sports film's reputation for formulaic predictability, as interrogative and complicating elements, sometimes explicit, sometimes residing in implicit subtexts, play against the most obvious closure and interpretation.

1. *CHARIOTS OF FIRE* (Hugh Hudson, 1981)

Praising famous men

Until the success of *Million Dollar Baby* in 2005, *Chariots of Fire* was only the second sports film to win the Best Picture Academy Award (1982), the first being *Rocky* (1976). *Chariots of Fire* is both like and unlike its predecessor; similar in its triumphant trajectory, but profoundly different in its Britishness, middle class milieu, and distant restrospection to the 'golden age' of amateurism. British films have succeeded in America, but rarely sports films, triply strange in their often un-American subjects, their less than full-on celebration of victorious heroism and tendencies to low-key irony. Two recent football films at a considerable tangent from *Bend It Like Beckham*, the only British sports film other than *Chariots of Fire* to achieve popular American success, support these generalisations – *The Damned United* based on the manager Brian Clough's failure to impose his will on the Leeds United team (the absolute obverse of every coach film from *Knute Rockne* to *Coach Carter*) – and *Best* dramatising the star's inability to control his life. In two celebrated earlier British films, *The Loneliness of the Long Distance Runner* (1962) and *This Sporting Life*, neither protagonist finds transcendence in sport. While the end of this discussion focuses on the ambiguities of a film that, for all its uplift, does not entirely disown these tendencies, *Chariots of Fire*'s retelling of Harold Abrahams' and Eric Liddell's 1924 Olympics victories, is predominantly heroic, as the text – the beginning of Ecclesiasticus, Chapter 44 – spoken at Abrahams' memorial service ('Let us [now] praise famous men and our fathers that begat us') and the film's most familiar images insist. The latter arrive conjured up by Lord Lindsay's words that he and 'young Aubrey Montagu are the only survivors who can close their eyes and remember that group of young men with hope in our hearts and wings on our heels', an invitation to the audience to share their memory, that recalls the opening of Olivier's *Henry V* (1944), though here the 'vasty fields of France' contract into the Stade Colombes. Aureoled by Vangelis' musical fusion of imperial reminiscence and soft synthesiser pop, the young men running delightedly by the sea in the white strip of Great Britain appear as the successors to the lost Great War generation mourned by the Master of Caius, but also as inheritors of the present ('and our fathers that begat us') since the film's athletic triumphs inevitably conjured up those of Sebastian Coe and Steve Ovett at the 1980 Moscow Olympics, the year before the film's release. Ecclesiasticus's catalogue of the famous – e.g. rulers, prophets, musicians, councillors, poets, the rich – would not be expected to contain sportsmen, but contemplation of their absence reminds us how, for the contemporary world (as for Pindar's fifth-century BC Greece), sportsmen and, nowadays, women are among those 'honoured in their generations', who 'have left a name behind'.

The template for the heroic (Pindaric?) sports film places obstacles in the protagonist's way – poverty, prejudice, race, illness and so on. *Chariots of Fire*, while following this pattern, subtly internalises its twin protagonists' impediments. Though Abrahams (Ben Cross) is pricked by the anti-Semitism in the Masters' and college porter's jokes and a student shouting 'Do it for Israel' before 'the College Dash', rather than obstructing it provokes his drive to achieve a central Englishness – as sporting hero – out of his father's Lithuanian Jewishness. This drive is given further expression 'between jest and earnest' in his love of Gilbert and Sullivan, with *HMS Pinafore*'s 'But in spite of all temptations/To belong to other nations/ He remains an Englishman!' genially staged. It is never suggested that his Jewishness creates barriers to Abrahams' athletic ambitions. Where obstruction exists is when hiring a professional trainer leads to conflict with the Masters of Caius and Trinity (Lindsay Anderson and John Gielgud), whose strictures damningly suggest the outsider's misapprehension of the codes of Englishness he aspires to, only for him to reject their fantasy of 'effortless superiority', answering 'I believe in the pursuit of excellence. I carry the future with me'. While Abrahams' Jewishness is entirely secular, a fervent evangelical Protestantism possesses the film's second centre, Liddell, creating the twin internalised obstacles he struggles with; first the view that his running conflicts with missionary responsibilities, second his belief that running on the Sabbath is wrong, an article of faith tested by the late announcement of Sunday competition in the 100 metres. Though the first dilemma is easily overcome ('*He* made me fast!'), the Sabbath's sanctity is not open to compromise, and just as Abrahams resists the Masters' blandishments, Liddell too holds firm in his 'little chat' with the Olympic Committee's Lords, and even the Prince of Wales, as they attempt to persuade him to run, with only Lord Lindsay's offer of his 400 metres place saving the day. Although the Olympic Committee aristocrats, with their

Abrahams triumphant
in *Chariots of Fire*

entirely social relation to religion, find Liddell incomprehensible, there is no way in which either his nationality or religion create an external, as distinct from internal, barrier to his ambitions. Equally neither athlete suffers from the class, economic or colour disadvantages that form more obvious barriers in other films.

Though the sports history film tends to greater factual accuracy than most biopics, *Chariots of Fire*, largely set nearly a century ago, takes considerable liberties with history, both with additions (e.g. Abrahams achieving the 'College Dash', and everything to do with Lord Lindsay) and suppressions (e.g. Abrahams' modest performance at the 1920 Olympics and Liddell's bronze in the 1924 200 metres). Most importantly, Liddell was never entered for the 100 metres since the Sunday scheduling was known months before. Recalling Lukác's defence of the overriding of fact in historical fictions, the shock of the announcement's invented lateness tests Liddell's principles more dramatically than the reality, while other changes clarify the narrative's main lines. Different in so many respects, the dual protagonists mirror each other in their will to win and refusal to compromise, though this symmetry coexists with differences which add to the film's richness – alongside the Jewish/Evangelical, secular/religious, and English/Scottish antitheses, the manufactured athlete versus the natural athlete, and the sportsman of the future (professionalisation) versus the sportsman of the past (amateurism). The film, following real life, denies the apparently promised Olympic 100 metres face-off between the two, leaving their rivalry finally unresolved, and, for all that the Englishman Abrahams is granted a degree of narrative predominance towards the end, both breast their different tapes equal winners, equally heroic.

Gentlemen and players

Chariots of Fire has been much analysed, but less as a sports film than as an early product of the radically conservative Thatcher era (1979–1990), that controversial time of change in British society. Though the film's key workers (screenwriter Colin Welland, producer David Puttnam, director Hugh Hudson) had left wing sympathies, and were unhappy with its patriotism being linked to the Falkland War (1982, only months after the Oscars), opposing interpretations of the film's ideological tendencies largely ignore the makers' overt affiliations. One dominant view finds an identification with Thatcherism in the athletes' clashes with traditional authority, Abrahams' espousing of professionalised efficiency, and the film's nationalism, while the other argues that, despite the film's critique of the reactionary Cambridge Masters, it is enamoured of the older order, with its imaging of Cambridge and framing use of Abrahams' establishment memorial service allying it to the nostalgic celebration of 'heritage' Englishness in films of the time. Given that such opposing arguments can be extrapolated from the same text, it is difficult to convincingly reduce its mixed impulses to either of those above. For instance, Liddell with his religion, Scottishness and empathy with the working class, is much more difficult to fit into a Thatcherite mold than Abrahams.

Approaching *Chariots of Fire* specifically as a sports film, one might find such ambivalences closely related to a thematic specific to its sports narrative, the meanings produced around the ethos of amateurism, crucial to de Coubertin's revival of the Olympic Games some thirty years before the film's events. As expressed in International Olympic Committee charters before the formal abolition of the long transgressed amateur/professional distinction in 1988, an amateur pursues an activity for love rather than for other rewards, especially monetary. Whatever the ideal, the Masters' 'chat' unconsciously reveals some of the amateur code's contradictions, in particular its élite class basis, with only the moneyed having the resources to train and play without 'broken time' payment for lost work compensating what the Master of Trinity calls the 'tradesman' (the issue which split the northern rugby league from the rugby union in England in 1895). It is thus no accident that three of the film's four central athletes are Cambridge students – Abrahams, Montague (in reality at Oxford) and Lord Lindsay – an obviously privileged group, with Liddell an Edinburgh undergraduate, though the film underplays this to differentiate him. The aristocratic Lord Lindsay (Nigel Havers), far from being criticised, as might seem logical to either a left wing or Thatcherite meritocratic view, is presented affirmatively, his view that the Olympics are 'fun', if rapidly sliding into the past, eliciting sympathy and providing an unforgettable testament to the enduring image of the 'English gentleman' as he perfects his hurdling technique by means of glasses brimful with champagne balanced on each hurdle (his model Lord Burghley, a winner in 1928, more prosaically used matchboxes). However much the College Masters are criticised for their snobbery, the film never criticises the athletes' privilege; indeed, whatever the inequalities of the system that enables them, as student-athletes they represent ideals of mind and body combined, athletes with 'hinterland' (that term attributed to the British politician Denis Healey, signifying interests beyond narrow specialisation).

Though the distant beginnings of later commercialisation and media domination of the Games are apparent in newspaper headlines, a newsreel of the Americans arriving and photographers and cine cameras inside the stadium, the small scale of the 1924 Games is striking, emphasised by the diminutive Merseyside stadium standing in for the Stade Colombes. Though occasional advertisements can be seen (Lipton's Tea, St Raphael *apéritif*, Pernod, Ovomaltine) the scale is so slight as to seem quaint, with footwear logo wars then undreamed of. Welland's early scripts explicitly condemned the contemporary takeover of the Games by big business and nationalism, one with an opening explicitly setting up a past/present comparison in which state controlled East German (DDR) winners represent a subversion of Olympic ideals. The film, as it less didactically emerged, leaves such comparisons implicit. But rather than simple nostalgia fantasising an impossible return to the past, Paris 1924 is a moment poised between past and future, holding in balance conflicting tendencies, like the beginning of Minnelli's great musical *Meet Me in St Louis* (1944) (that city incidentally the site of the 1904 Olympics, though they are never mentioned as one of the Exposition's attractions) where horse-drawn vehicles and new-fangled automobiles idyllically coexist, though logically the latter predict the former's obsolescence. Here Liddell's unambiguous amateurism, Abrahams' professionalisation (as distinct from professionalism), paralleled by the Americans' multi coach-directed training, and Lindsay's privileged aristocratic *sprezzatura* stand side by side, though the first and last are doomed to disappear, with the professional coach Mussabini's exclusion from the stadium both condemning the amateur code's rigidities and representing the forces of future professionalism still held in check. The frozen moment allows critique of the outmodedness of the extreme amateur ethos in the modern world and approval of Abrahams' boundary breaking, without following up its later consequences. Equally, while the excitements of international competition so fundamental to most modern sports, are captured in the British-American battles, there is still space for the American Scholz's act, after warning his compatriot against his coach's underestimation of Liddell, of giving Liddell the note of support which he carries in the race, one of several reminders of sport as a personal rather than national endeavour (also enacted notably in Mussabini's and Abrahams' post-victory celebration).

In *The Four Minute Mile* (1989), set 30 years later, made just after the IOC erased the amateur/professional distinction, the 1954 Empire Games are celebrated as 'the last point in time... when men and women still compete to the utmost of their capacity, not for glory, not for gold but for the sheer joy of doing something as well or better than it has been done before'. Actually things are more complex than the official's speech suggests in a narrative where certainly glory is a factor (as in *Chariots of Fire*), and where doing things 'better than... before' raises questions, comparable to Abrahams' hiring of Mussabini, about 'pacing', i.e. using runners not trying to win but to help break a record. Ironically, when Bannister's coach Franz Stampfl tells him 'Pacing is here to stay,' he adds 'Don't worry about Abrahams', who is now identified with the Amateur Athletic Association, arguing against pacing-aided records.

The Four Minute Mile makes overt what is implicit in *Chariots of Fire,* that for all the amateur code's hypocrisies (with the American Santee, the prime rival of both Bannister and Landy, banned for a year from competing overseas for accepting a $200 camera as a prize), something precious will be lost with the irresistible march towards full professionalism, crystallised around the figure of Bannister, and to a lesser degree Landy, individuals who, like Abrahams and Liddell, practiced a sport to the highest level as well as doing something else, raising the question of whether the ideal of mind and body represented particularly by Bannister's medical studies (he became a distinguished neurologist) could ever be possible again.

Winning and losing

Within the heroic narrative exist moments inviting more unsettling responses than elsewhere. Three stand out. Liddell's sermon on the Sunday of the 100 metres heats, Abrahams' confession to Aubrey Montague before, and his retracted behaviour after, his victory. Liddell's text, from Isaiah 40 ('They shall run and not be weary. They shall walk and not faint'), recalls his address to the spectators after one of his earlier races ('I want to compare faith with running in a race'). As he speaks images are intercut from the stadium, predominantly of athletes failing, collapsing and falling, Mussabini chastising Abrahams for errors in the unshown 200 metres in which he finished last, and an exhausted Montague finishing the steeplechase sixth, the contestants soiled with mud from the water jump.

Elements of Liddell's text – 'Behold the nations are as a drop in the bucket and are counted as the small dust in the balance' – fit awkwardly with the buoyant nationalism of the Great Britain v USA athletics battle, as do Lord Sutherland's unexpectedly barbed comments to Lord Cadogan about nationalism and the Great War, and to Birkenhead about 'guilty national pride'. Other ambivalent moments foreground Abrahams. While massaged by Mussabini, Abrahams tells Aubrey Montague that he is his 'most complete man', possessing the secret of 'contentment' whereas he himself is 'forever in pursuit, and I don't know what I'm chasing'. His concluding 'I'm almost too frightened to win' clearly signifies more than pre-race nerves, for when victory celebrations continue in the dressing room, Abrahams just packs his suitcase, oblivious to them. As Montague moves to offer him champagne, Lindsay intervenes, implying that for Abrahams winning is as much the problem as the solution: 'One of these days you're going to win yourself and it's pretty difficult to swallow.' Moments later Abrahams exits without a word. The initially estranging, momentarily unplaceable close up of Abrahams looking tormented, belatedly situated as the opening shot of his and Mussabini's drunken celebrations, adds to these suggestions, as do his grimace and agonised gesture in rising to toast his coach. And earlier, watching Liddell win, he is seen in another close up, gaunt, perhaps thinking that circumstances have prevented himself and Liddell deciding who is faster, thus compromising his victory. Further, though present at trackside celebrating Liddell's win, he is absent from the team's celebrations as they board a victory vehicle. As regards Lindsay's gnomic wisdom about the difficulty of winning, the British Beijing 2008 gold medal cyclist Victoria Pendleton confessed that her victory left her depressed, 'sad and numb' (Dineen and O'Connor 2009). Such depression is more likely to affect the athlete whose whole being is temporarily concentrated on their event, e.g. an Abrahams, than the athlete who, even if as fiercely competitive as Liddell, because of his or her worldview, cannot have unreal expectations of the meanings of winning. (Liddell tells the spectators after an earlier win, 'You feel elation when the winner breasts the tape but how long does that last?') The events of 1924 close with the romantic plot consolidated as Sybil, Abrahams' fiancée, meets the returning hero's train, but even this has curious undertones. She waits until it seems that Harold is not among the passengers, and only then does he belatedly appear, walking towards her embrace, suggesting a hesitancy about rejoining the more complex world beyond athletics, a moment which segues into the affirmations of the memorial service singing of 'Jerusalem' (with none of the ironies of its earlier use in *The Loneliness of the Long Distance Runner*) and the closing repetition of the seaside run images – but, as Whannel, curiously the only writer on the film to hint at these dissonances, notes, without 'a magical resolution or a utopian glow' (2008: 91).

2. *FIELD OF DREAMS* (Phil Alden Robinson, 1989)

Dreamtime

> For the field is full of shades as I near the shadowy coast
> And a ghostly batsman plays to the bowling of a ghost…
> — Francis Thompson, 'At Lord's' (Thompson 2001: 484)

In *Field of Dreams* an American sports film abandons the agonistic plot that drives Hollywood's version of the genre. This is a baseball film – even a meta-baseball film – without major league or World Series showdowns. In fact, the only league games glimpsed are fragments, as when Ray and Terence Mann visit Fenway Park where the play is pushed into the background by the voice commanding 'Ease his pain' and by 'Moonlight' Graham's uncanny scoreboard appearance. When Ray Kinsella (Kevin Costner) hears a voice in his Iowa cornfield telling him 'If you build it, he

'Shoeless Joe' in *Field of Dreams*

will come', 'he' or 'He' turns out to be nothing so obvious as an unknown rookie to lead a team to success. Instead the film inflects into a quest narrative ('Build what? Who's "he"?'), only the first stage of which is Ray's conviction that he has to build a ballpark for the return of 'Shoeless' Joe Jackson, the greatest of the notorious Chicago White Sox who took bribes to throw the 1919 World Series. The appearance of the long dead Joe (Ray Liotta) only initiates the next stage as the voice lays two more commands on Ray, 'Ease his Pain' ('What the hell does that mean? What pain? Whose pain?') and 'Go the Distance', impelling him to track down a black writer from the sixties, Terence Mann (James Earl Jones), that he and his wife, Annie, admire. The narrative then sends Ray and Mann on a time-warped search for 'Moonlight' Graham (Burt Lancaster), an old player whose major league career was cut off after the one game he played in without ever batting, and who later became a beloved smalltown Minnesota doctor. Ray and Terence Mann, finally heading back to Iowa, give a lift to the deceased Archie Graham's younger incarnation, enabling him to fulfil his older self's ambition of facing a big league pitcher, while Ray's late, estranged father, John, also appears at the ground as his youthful ball playing self. By the film's close, then, the gnomic commands have expanded their meaning – the 'he' who will come, and whose pain will be eased, spreading to include 'Shoeless' Joe, Terence Mann, 'Moonlight' Graham, Ray's father, John, and

Ray himself, not to mention the visitors to Ray's ballpark, the first of whose cars approach as the film ends.

Wes D. Gehring's book *Mr Deeds Goes to Yankee Stadium: Baseball Films in the Capra Tradition* unashamedly celebrates as central to the sub-type a tradition of populist 'Capraesque' sentiment and nostalgia, powerful enough to turn Bernard Malamud's fable of hubristic defeat, *The Natural*, into unalloyed optimism in the film version. Such films include the sentiment-soaked *The Pride of The Yankees* and *The Babe Ruth Story*, as well as those anticipating *Field of Dreams'* baseball fantasy, most importantly *Angels in the Outfield* (1951) in which 'Heavenly Choir 9' made up of deceased greats invisibly help the struggling Pittsburgh Pirates. This tradition links baseball to rural, small-town American virtues, to 'timeless' tradition, to what Gehring defines as 'second chances', to faith in some benign ecumenical metaphysics (symbolised by the committee of a protestant clergyman, a catholic priest and a rabbi who investigate the existence of the angels in *Angels in the Outfield*), and to familial and generational stability – e.g the images of father and son playing catch that end both *The Natural* (1984) and also *Field of Dreams* (Gehring 2004). Contrastingly, Vivian Sobchak in 'Baseball in the post-American Cinema, or Life in the Minor Leagues' sees the baseball film more jaundicedly, viewing its contemporary versions as reacting to fading confidence in white centrality and a pure (white, male) American identity in a multicultural era either with a regressive denial of change or a reluctant charting of unwelcome fracturings. Sobchak's argument views the sports world, in which much mainstream American sport is now dominated by Afro-American and other non-white players, as a microcosm of larger trends, with films about baseball – historically the sport with the 'most prominent role in the American imaginary' and the most prone to idealisation – resisting these changes by locating the game 'in a hermetic, timeless, oneiric vision of America that always has a white Middle American Casey at bat' (1997: 181, 191). In such a context, *Field of Dreams*, 'a film promiscuously nostalgic and illusionary' (1997: 185), cultivating the oneiric, the timeless, featuring white players only, and set in the overwhelmingly white 'heartland' of Iowa, is viewed harshly beneath its appeal to that innocent common fantasy of sports followers of imagining resurrected greats playing again. But *Field of Dreams* can hardly import black players into the 1919 White Sox, and if accused of choosing that past as a way of cancelling the hybrid present, could answer that the 1919 White Sox occupy too crucial a place in the history of American sport for a recall of them to be seen simply in such terms. Presumably John Sayles' more analytical film about them, *8 Men Out*, could not reasonably be read in the same way. To say this is not to banish all such problematics from the film, but *Field of Dreams* does make major changes to its source, W. Kinsella's novel *Shoeless Joe* (1982), which is certainly open to the above critiques, omitting, for instance, its symptomatic scene of racial panic where Ray, on his way to Comiskey Park, strays into a threatening black South Chicago environment. By contrast the film (1989) is sensitive to the issues later formulated by Sobchak (in 1997), not only augmenting the parts of Ray's wife Annie and daughter Karin, but replacing J. D. Salinger as the author sought by Ray with the invented black writer Terence Mann, a softened composite of Ralph Ellison and James Baldwin out of Salinger, who, like the latter, has become a non-publishing recluse, in his case disillusioned with the decline of 1960s radicalism. He is also a baseball fan who dreamed of playing for the Brooklyn Dodgers alongside Jackie Robinson, but has not watched a game since 1958, the year after the Brooklyn Dodgers left Ebbets Field for Los Angeles, a pivotal moment in the overriding of local traditions by financially-driven franchising in American sport. Mann, remembered by Ray and Annie as an inspiring figure of a hopeful time, is defended by Annie when the reactionary Mrs Gasnik attacks his books at a PTA meeting as 'smut' and 'filth' and advocating 'mongrelisation of the race' (Sobchak writes of the white American middle class fear of being 'hybridized'). Marking his metamorphosis from Salinger, Mann is discovered by Ray in a markedly Jewish neighbourhood, a conjunction of Jewish and Afro-American mitigating the film's otherwise WASP predominance. Further, though the film, like the novel, clasps at baseball as, somewhat tendentiously, the only thing that has not changed in America to invoke a vision of a better past to guide a better future, the film substantially tones down the novel's religiosity ('take the word of baseball and begin to talk it... The word of salvation is baseball') – a rhetoric without the ironies of Annie Savoy's (Susan Sarandon) celebration of 'the Church of Baseball' in *Bull Durham*, or of Philip Roth's grotesquely comic, dystopian use of the game to chart the failures of modern American history in *The Great American Novel*. Additionally, the past alluded to is partly disconnected from the novel's pre-1914 imaginings and recentred on the 1960s which are much alluded to verbally – and visually and aurally – in the Warhol Marilyn and Jim Dine Heart prints in Ray and Annie's house, and a

Patsy Cline recording. This means that when Mann, who speaks familiarly of 'Bobby', 'Martin' and 'Tricky Dicky', argues that people visiting the ground will feel they have been 'dipped in memory', memory is in part identified with an era of change more dynamic than the novel's static 'home-canned preserves, ice cream made in a wooden freezer' vision.

Dream and reality: 'Is this heaven?' 'No, it's Iowa.'

Cinematic allusions both underline the narrative as fantasy and its difference from its novelistic source. Annie jokes that Terence Mann had a childhood baseball bat named 'Rosebud', and Ray's daughter watches the film *Harvey* (Henry Koster, 1950) on television. The play on *Citizen Kane* (Orson Welles, 1941) recognises the narrative's nostalgia for childhood innocence, while the fleeting introduction of James Stewart's benign alcoholic fantasist and his imaginary friend, acknowledges its foundation in subjective desire. As one of the eight disappears into the unknown, mimicking the Wicked Witch of the West in *The Wizard of Oz* (Victor Fleming, 1939), he cries out in mock anguish 'I'm melting, I'm melting'. And as Doc Graham returns to that unknown zone, his farewell echoes the Gipper's deathbed exhortation in *Knute Rockne* with 'Win one for me one day, will you, boys?'

Field of Dreams is the ultimate refinement and apotheosis of the fan film. Neither Ray nor Terence Mann have played at even minors level. Joe, on the contrary, has been a great professional star, from whom one would expect pragmatic attitudes, but double exile from the sport, first in life, then in death, makes him return like one of Wallace Stevens' ghosts 'that would have wept to step barefoot into reality' (Stevens 1954: 423). He is a dreamy lover and preserver of the game like Ray and Terence – 'Man, I did love this game' – celebrating its smells and sounds, and everything associated with it including even the travelling, trains and hotels, finally saying 'I'd have played for food money ... shoot, I'd play for nothing', an opportunity which he is indeed given.

Like the most satisfying utopian imaginings *Field of Dreams* does not wholly forget the compromised reality it transcends, hinting at the problems and dissonances that the dream all but dissolves. These take two primary forms: (i) the paradox of the purer past being identified with a criminal enterprise; and (ii) the literal cost of the dream world, the economics of ideality. A third occurrence, soothing rather than unsettling, at one with the curious identification of the traditional baseball film with an optimistic American metaphysic, allows Terence Mann at the narrative's end to enter the mysterious space from which the players commute, promising to write a story on it on his return.

To redefine (i), the question is how the vision of a purer past provided by Ray's ballpark can be so closely associated with American sport's most notorious fix? Ray states his belief in Joe's innocence, pointing to his spotless playing record in the thrown series, asserting that the building of his park is to 'right an old wrong'. But, even if Joe played cleanly in the series, he still accepted bribes. The choice of Ray Liotta to play him is hardly straightforward, since that actor, even before *Goodfellas* (Martin Scorsese, 1990), was identified with deviant characters, his roles in *Something Wild* (Jonathan Demme, 1986) and *The Lonely Lady* (Peter Sasdy, 1986) before *Field of Dreams* both being variations on psychopathy/criminality, so that his already darkling persona must cast some shadow on Joe. Ray makes no extenuating arguments for the other seven, yet when Joe asks for them to be allowed in, Ray agrees unquestioningly. Neither in the source novel nor the film can Ray bring himself to question Joe about 1919, an evasion which might well suggest that he has unspoken doubts. The nearest Joe comes to speaking about the crime is extremely oblique. When he questions Ray about his ground's floodlights (never having played under lights himself, though living until 1950 he must have been aware of them), Ray explains that the owners built them to draw bigger crowds. Joe's reply is the single word 'Owners!', implying that they have, as ever, put profit before the game, and that it was the greed of the White Sox owner, Komiskey, that caused the fix — basically the line taken in *8 Men Out*. If the building of Ray's ballpark 'right[s] an old wrong' — i.e. Joe's banning by Judge Landis — a second meaning attaches itself to the words, the 'old wrong' being that committed by the eight, who are now readmitted to the game despite their guilt, to play again in circumstances that have expelled the conditions of their fall. This is a kind of utopia in the later vein of Pierre Bourdieu, restoring 'those values which the world of sport proclaims and which are very like the values of art and science (non-commercial, ends in themselves, disinterested, valuing fair play and the 'way the game is played' as opposed to sacrificing everything for results)' (Giulianotti 2005; 167, quoting Bourdieu). This paradoxical yoking together of the paradisical and the criminal recognises that an Edenic past wholly innocent of corruption is as unlocatable in sport as in anything else, and that any apparently found will prove to be a compromised utopia, needing, amidst its cherishing for lost simplicities, forgiveness for its role in initiating the realities of present day sport, its commercialism, its cheating, its greed; specifically regarding baseball, the recent steroid scandals involving high profile 'juicers' such as Barry Bonds and Mark McGwire, with claims that even revered players of the past like Babe Ruth and Mickey Mantle experimented with testosterone, and the hugely unpopular strike of enormously-paid players in 1994–95.

(ii) From the point that Ray builds the ballpark on one of his cornfields his ownership of his farm is threatened. With it no longer bringing in enough to pay the mortgage, Mark, Annie's yuppie brother, pressures him to sell it in return for guaranteed possession of the house. Thus the building of the park is deeply embedded in financial problematics; the vision, like the structures sustaining professional sport, has to be paid for. Even if in this case salaries can be waived, it still has to attract revenue to sustain its vivified Cooperstown. The solution is a $20 metaphysical theme park entrance fee (reminiscent of the contained benign capitalism of Capra's *It's a Wonderful Life*, 1946), purified by its being suggested by a child, Karin, before being taken up and endorsed by Terence Mann, who we understand to be a critic of unfettered capitalism. The reality principle is thus not wholly abandoned (even if astronomical salaries are), but softened to something like the rural 1930s idyll lived in their youths by Archie Graham and Ray's father, John – 'I heard that all through the Midwest they have towns with teams and some places they even give you a day job so that you can play ball nights [i.e. summer evenings presumably] and weekends.' When the young Archie Graham says this, Ray replies, 'We're going some place kinda like that' – like but not quite identical because the players are unpaid, because the spectators pay, and because the game – despite Joe's 'Owners!' – is played under lights, with the first spectators arriving as night falls.

(iii) The baseball film's attraction to fantasy presents the paranormal benignly – those guardian 'angels in the outfield' – even to the point where the game (associated with summer, childhood, innocence, pastoral, the myth of American exceptionalism in which the fantasy of baseball's autochthonous American origins, despite its obvious parentage in the English children's game of rounders, plays an important part), becomes a vehicle for the tenor of American metaphysical optimism. Whenever they have finished playing on Ray's field, the players walk from the field and disappear into a metaphysical zone of some sort of afterlife. Just before the narrative's close, Joe suddenly invites Terence Mann to accompany them across the border. Ray, upset, angrily argues that it is he who should be going because he built the ground, protesting 'You guys are guests in my corn', and is rebuked by Joe for behaving like an owner ('What's in it for me?') The upshot is that it is Terence Mann the writer who goes ('There is something out there, Ray, and if I have the courage to go through with this what a story it'll make'). In other words, rather more definite than the film's hopeful indefinites, Terence Mann is to become a metaphysical reporter whose article on return will presumably clarify the existence of a personal God and the meaning of life, though neither Joe nor any of the other players has anything to say about the afterlife, except for one who implies a smoking ban, or perhaps just a lack of cigarettes. Another more secularised reason for Terence Mann being chosen might be that, in his admission to the baseball beyond, he acts as a surrogate for Jackie Robinson and many before him in the negro baseball leagues prevented from playing in the majors before segregation ended, another instance of the film's more liberal inflection of its source's social implications.

3. *LAGAAN* (Ashutosh Gowariker, 2001)

Ramachandra Guha's *A Corner of a Foreign Field: The Indian History of a British Sport* (2002) describes itself as telling 'the story of Indian cricket ... through the master categories of race, caste, religion and nation', in this constituting a paradigm of the examination of sport and social context. As India, with its billion-plus population and increasing international presence, has become world cricket's financial centre, two of its characteristic cultural phenomena, cricket and the popular cinema, have embraced, resulting in a recent output of cricket films aimed at internal and diasporic audiences – *Iqbal* (Nagesh Kukunoor, 2005), *Stumped* (Gaurav Pandey, 2003), *Say Salaam India* (Subhash Kapoor, 2007), *Victory* (Pritam Guha, 2009), and the Tamil 'street cricket' film *Chennai 60028* (Venkat Prabhu, 2007). *Lagaan,* though, has been more than an Indian success, nominated for Best Foreign Film Academy Award (2002), widely exhibited and praised overseas, and seen as a key text in the recent Bollywood/Western cinema confluence. Like Guha's history, it deploys race, nation, religion and caste in its story of a wager imposed by a British army officer, Captain Russell (Paul Blackthorne), on the villagers of Champaner; that if they beat the local occupying army at the English game of cricket, then their crippling *lagaan* (tax) will be lifted, but tripled if they lose. The narrative follows Bhuvan's (Amir Khan) seemingly impossible task of training a team, helped by Russell's sympathetic sister, Elizabeth (Rachel Shelley), culminating in the epic match won by the villagers.

Cricket films, English and Indian

In his authoritative essay on cricket and film, 'What's Happening to England?', Charles Barr writes of the 'slackly indulgent' treatment of the game in what was, until *Lagaan*, the best known cricket feature, *The Final Test*, a judgement difficult to dispute (Barr 2004: 116). If the traditional American baseball film's besetting vice is sentimentality, that of its less frequent English cricket equivalent is self-regarding middle-class whimsy (*The Final Test*'s complacent bafflement of the American senator attending the test match exemplifies this), though the latter characteristic is wholly missing from three recent English cricket documentaries, *Fire in Babylon* (2010), *Afghan Cricket Club: Out of the Ashes* (2011) and *From the Ashes* (2011), all more concerned with the sport's complex social relations than with regressive mythologies. In contrast to the older English cricket film, Barr instances *The Go-Between* as vividly utilising the game's dramatic possibilities and historical associations with class complexities, which, along with race, are also fundamental to Horace Ové's *Playing Away,* discussed earlier.

But over the past decade India has been the chief source of fictional cricket films. These productions, however different formally, resemble traditional American baseball films more than their English cricket equivalents – in their populism, their national rather than class allegory, and the optimism of their success plots. The Indian cricket film differs from both English and American prototypes in shunning nostalgia, identifying the game with the synergies of Indian modernity rather than tradition (indeed all the Indian films, except *Lagaan*, centre on the faster, less complex, modern limited overs game, and even the three day game in *Lagaan* slips into one day rules near its end). Basic success stories dominate: e.g. *Iqbal* (poor, rural, deaf and dumb Muslim becomes fast bowler for India) and *Say Salaam India* (three schoolboys, Hindu, Muslim, Sikh, defeat socially advantaged opponents). In dramatising opportunity beyond the great conurbations

The great game under way in *Lagaan*

they underwrite one of contemporary India's grand narratives, though this cricket/nation equation is less benign in *Stumped*, set during the simultaneous 1999 cricket World Cup and the India/Pakistan war in Kargil, with cricket stars such as Sachin Tendulkar and Kapil Dev extolling the Indian military. What differentiates *Lagaan* from these lesser films, apart from its greater ambitions and subtler workings of the cricket/nation dyad, is its pre-modern setting, though clearly its Raj scenario looks forward to India's emergence into independence and modernity.

In popular Indian cinema's '*masala*' hybridity, song and dance are central, not only aesthetically but financially, with music rights involving major playback (dubbing) stars like *Lagaan*'s (Alka Yagnik, Asha Bhosle and others) underwriting up to a quarter of a film's budget. *Lagaan*'s musical numbers are not specifically about the sport (like, say, 'O'Brien to Ryan to Goldberg' in the musical *Take Me Out to the Ballgame*), though in *Stumped* one celebrates cricket stars, 'Rahul Dravid, Tendulkar ... This is how Gavaskar started.' Rather, *Lagaan*'s numbers melodramatise the action's implications and the love plot's vicissitudes, with the usual embroidery of Hindu religious and mythological allusions.

Race and nation

'The year is 1893. Champaner, a small village in Central India', the film's historical voice over intones. In the pre-credit sequence a coin bearing Queen Victoria's head, dated 1877 (the year she became 'Empress of India'), spins like the coin tossed for choice of innings at the beginning of a cricket match and falls on a map of India in a central region somewhere between Berar and Bihar, though the credits imply the film was shot in Gujerat. Any confusion is deliberate, suggesting, via allusions in the film's subtitle *Once Upon a Time in India* to Sergio Leone's *Once upon a Time in the West* (1984) and *Once upon a Time in America* (1984), that this is once upon a place in India, the less specific the better. Though it was in cities like Calcutta and Bombay (where in 1885 the Congress Party was formed) that Indian nationalism was first promulgated largely by English educated Indians, and Indians first played cricket in imitation of their rulers, the film's rural setting allows a more basic drama to be staged.

Because the village is hardly cosmopolitan, the film cannot, like the women's hockey film *Chak De India!*, set in the urban present, bring far-flung representatives of the hugely heterogeneous nation together, making the team a microcosm of a multiregional but united India. In that film, coach Kabir Khan, asserting that 'I cannot hear or see the names of states, I can only hear the name of one country – India', asks the girls to introduce themselves, which they do in a way which displeases him – 'Balbir Kaub, Punjab', 'Komal Chautala, Hariyana' and so on until one takes the point, 'Vidya Sharma, *India*'. Instead, *Lagaan* presents representative village types: the boy who plays *gilli danda* (a children's game with remote similarities to cricket), the local doctor, a chicken farmer (his reactions honed by catching chickens on the run), a slingshot expert whose skills suggest he can bowl, the fortune teller, the blacksmith and so on, a Muslim, a Sikh and an untouchable, a magnificent eleven rather than seven, with that eastern turned western allusively saluted as the team march towards the camera, cricket bats held like rifles the night before the great game.

Their opponents, the British army occupiers, are arrogant and prejudiced, with Captain Russell embodying their worst aspects. But, despite the hate they inspire through their mistreatment of the villagers, the English, at least some of them, reveal another side, the legacy of Victorian sport's codes of fair play, even though their relation to them is often hypocritical when playing 'lesser breeds'. The English umpires from Khanpur act with scrupulous fairness, allowing Goli's slingshot bowling because no rule forbids it, and calling the no ball that swings the game. Colonel Boyer, in particular, praises the novices' good play and sympathises when they have bad luck. The most sympathetic of the English, Elizabeth Russell, teaches the villagers the game's basics. Justice, and sympathy for India, motivate her, but it soon becomes clear that she has fallen for Bhuvan, an unconsummated love given richest expression in the musical number after the temple of Krishna and Radha scene where Bhuvan explains to her the divine pair's ideal extra-marital love, in which she fantasises both taking the heroine Gauri's (Gracie Singh) place in the village and Bhuvan in British army uniform, waltzing with her at a regimental ball. In this reversal of the colonial love plot of white man and native woman (and where it is unclear how much Bhuvan recognises Elizabeth's passion), separation is inevitable, as for Edwina Mountbatten and Nehru, to whom it may knowingly allude. Indeed, their farewell, Bhuvan's 'Memsahib, we will never forget what you've done for us', and the voice over's 'she did not marry and remained Bhuvan's Radha all her life' allegorise India's and Britain's post-Independence relationship 'neither united nor separate' – shared democracy, law, the English language, Shakespeare, traditions of bureaucracy, railways, the large British Indian Diaspora, with – since Bhuvan is more desired by Elizabeth than she by him – future power relations much altered in India's favour. The film, beginning as a 'race film' (featuring serious racial prejudice), ends as a 'cross-cultural film', with a degree of reconciliation. The sharing of course extends to cricket, with remarks during the game prophesying India's future success – Colonel Boyer's 'Do you realise that we could have on our hands, a bloody situation where there'll be cricket matches all over the damned subcontinent?' and the civil servant who says admiringly 'this country could have a great future at this game'.

With the English eleven's defeat, the *lagaan* is lifted, the army abandons Champanar, and Captain Russell is sent in disgrace to Africa, this ending, after the smaller 'tryst with destiny' (India taking up cricket, the villagers defeating the colonists), foreshadowing the occupiers' final exit and the greater 'tryst with destiny' of Nehru's Independence speech on 15 August, 1947.

Religion and caste

Ismail, a Muslim, has been Bhuvan's childhood rival at *gilli danda*. When he volunteers to play ('Allah commands it'), Bhuvan welcomes him, implicitly invoking Muslim cricketers picked for, even captaining, post-partition India (e.g. Mansoor Ali Khan Pataudi, Mohammad Azharuddin). The inescapable context here is the conflict between India and Pakistan and between India's 140 million Muslims and its overwhelming Hindu majority, exacerbated by friction over Kashmir, and the extremist ideologies of Islamic fundamentalism and Hindu nationalism. The latter, in the period before *Lagaan*, dangerously revived the old dispute over the Ayodhya mosque, eventually destroyed by Hindu communalists in 1992, an act worsening a volatile situation, in which cricket has been implicated, both through the suspension of India/Pakistan matches at times of worst relations and subcontinental 'table tennis diplomacy' using the game to rebuild bridges, but with dangerously heightened nationalism surrounding the matches. The Mumbai Bollywood industry, though the fount of Hindi cinema, is a zone of creative multiculturalism, using many Muslim personnel, including the three phenomenally popular contemporary male stars, Amir Khan, Sharukh Khan and Salman Khan. Thus, though Amir Khan plays a Hindu hero, the fact that a Muslim can represent a Hindu on screen can be seen as questioning Hindu/Muslim essentialisms.

Lagaan's other religious outsider is Deva Singh Sodhi, a fierce figure who learned cricket serving in the British army, a reminder of Sikh players for India (e.g. Bishan Bedi Singh and Harbhajan Singh). His presence not only restates India's religious diversity, but the precariousness of Nehru's secular state. Punjabi Sikh-on-Hindu violence marked the decade preceding *Lagaan*, linked to demands for Sikh independence and resulting in the army operation against the armed rebels in the Golden Temple at Amritsar, which led to Indira Gandhi's assassination by her Sikh bodyguards, which in turn precipitated major Hindu violence against Sikhs.

The third outsider, Kachra, the untouchable, appears when, at practice, the ball lands where he stands isolated by his pollution. Ordered to return it, he bowls it back with his crippled arm, revealing a spin bowling talent which convinces Bhuvan he should be in the team. Kachra reminds aficionados of Baghwat Chandrasekhar, whose polio afflicted arm bowled India to a historic first series victory in England in 1971, but also of India's first great bowler, Palwankar Baloo, seventeen at the time of the film's fictional game, who, though an untouchable, forced his way into the representative Hindu side and even the 1911 All India side that toured England, despite many objections and humiliations. When the villagers react with horror to Bhuvan's choosing Kachra, Bhuvan, denouncing their inhumanity, reminds them how an untouchable ferryman aided Lord Krishna, and persuades them to incorporate the outcast. As with the issues condensed around Ismail and Deva Singh, caste discrimination has not disappeared with modernity, remaining, despite government actions, a fundamental Indian reality (as demonstrated by caste's controversial inclusion in the 2010 census), still causing major conflicts and atrocities. Like the war film's patrol group, Bhuvan's team is a synecdoche of disparate religions, interests and classes united, an optimistic vision of the healed nation, and simultaneously a reminder of its fault lines.

Playing the game

A contest of epic length (78 minutes from preliminaries to victory celebrations, 58 of actual play) in a film of epic length (224 minutes), the match in *Lagaan*, like other extended fictional contests, e.g. those which end *The Longest Yard* (Robert Aldrich, 1974) (American football), *Old Scores* (rugby union), and *Escape to Victory* (football), fulfils four basic criteria. (i) It must be staged convincingly, according to current standards of representation. (ii) It must reduce the game, however complex, to essentials for audiences unfamiliar with it. (iii) At the same time, it must contain enough authentic elements to interest knowledgeable viewers. (iv) Beyond the usual strong identification with one side (villagers v British army, Allies v Nazis, sadistic guards v prisoners, with *Old Scores* exceptionally asking for identification with both New Zealand and Wales) the audience must be connected to the game through particular identifications with central narrative characters.

As regards (ii), when in *Lagaan* Deva Singh summarises his knowledge of cricket, he says, 'Two things... . When I throw the ball it is to shatter all three stumps. And when I hit the ball it is to smash it to pieces' a hyperbole of how the game (or any game with rules more complex than boxing, racing, jumping or throwing) must be presented. That all such games, especially team sports, have aspects opaque to the uninitiated is the basis of the scene where the villagers spy on the army cricketers and make comical, obviously mistaken assumptions. A way of consolidating audience comprehension is for a broadcast commentary to accompany the game (*Escape to Victory, Old Scores, The Longest Yard* intermittently). *Lagaan* ingeniously uses the Indian crowd's ignorance of the new game to have important details explained to them (and the film's uninitiated audiences) by megaphone announce-

ments. As for (iii), with the game reduced to basics, more specialised material may be developed, with, in *Lagaan*, the army batsmen accurately imitating the high late Victorian/Edwardian style of batting, and batsmen given
out leg before wicket, which the uninitiated audience accepts, even if not
fully understanding, going with the narrative flow. Similarly, in *Any Given
Sunday* anyone not familiar with American football's complex rules will not
understand why Julian Washington runs into touch near the game's end (in
all other forms of football this would be self-defeating), but will gather from
the coach's reactions and what follows that it is to his team's advantage.

As for (iv), in *The Go-Between*'s cricket match, the focal character, the
boy, Leo, plays with and against the two adult figures to whom he feels
conflicting loyalties, Lord Trimmingham and the farmer Ted Burgess, rivals
for Marian, with whom he is himself childishly in love. The game is structured round all three males (with Marian and her mother important figures
among the spectators) so that its events signify doubly, with Leo, in taking
the catch that dismisses Ted, auguring Ted's losing Marian and his later
suicide. In *Lagaan*, Bhuvan and Captain Russell, the opposing captains, are
always central. It is Russell who triumphantly catches Bhuvan off the last ball
apparently to defeat the villagers, only to realise that he has overstepped
the boundary and that a six has won the match. Lesser identifications are
encouraged with the various village players (Kachra for his untouchability,
Tipu for his youth, Arjan for his eccentricity, etc.), for instance with Kachra
when he loses his ability to spin the ball, and then when he suddenly
regains his powers, and with Arjan when, taunted by the English players,
he loses control, with Yardley, the vicious fast bowler intent on injuring the
Indian batsmen, a figure of secondary anti-identification. Constantly seeking emotional engagement, the camera seeks out important characters in
the crowd, here Elizabeth, the Rajah, Gauri, Bhuvan's mother and Colonel
Boyer, for their reactions. (In *Old Scores*, the Welsh and New Zealand rugby
union chiefs and the family of a player with affiliations to both nations, in
The Longest Yard the power-mad Warden and various non-playing prisoners,
in *Escape to Victory* the British and Nazi officers.) In order both to break up
the sports action and underline its connection to larger narrative meanings,
all these sequences contain off-field scenes, set in the half-time intervals
of the football games (in *The Longest Yard* the Warden blackmails Phil into
throwing the game, in *Escape to Victory* the escape tunnel is completed,
but the team decide to finish the game, in *Old Scores* the Welsh President

arranges for the antique ball 'Old Lucky' to be brought into play). In *Lagaan,* where two nights pass between the three days of play, on the first night Lakha's treachery is discovered, the villagers turn against him, and Bhuvan allows him to redeem himself; while on the second the women revive the men's hopes with their hymn 'O Saviour pure of essence'.

4. *ANY GIVEN SUNDAY* (Oliver Stone, 1999)

Any Given Sunday is one of the few films to approach contemporary professional sport – here American football – as an institution, a commodity, advertising and media business constructed around the game, a superstructure so influential that it becomes infrastructural, effecting changes on the sport itself. Others are the Australian Rules film *The Club, Jerry Maguire* (Cameron Crowe, 1996) with its rather sentimental dealings with the very contemporary phenomenon of sports agency, *This Sporting Life*, *The Damned United*, *North Dallas Forty, Major League* (David S. Ward, 1999), where the owner actually wants the team to lose so that the franchise can be moved, *Mr Baseball* (Fred Schepisi, 1992), the ice hockey film *Slapshot* (George Roy Hill, 1977), where the team is merely the owner's dispensable tax write off, *The Final Winter* (Brian Andrews and Jane Forrest, 2007), centring on new commercial priorities changing Australian rugby league in the 1980s, and *Moneyball*, concerned with innovatory methods of countering economic disparities between the richest baseball clubs and the poorer. However, compared to these, Stone's film more unrelentingly portrays sport in the age of corporations, franchises, media saturation and commodification. If this suggests sustained critique, like that of the least idealising of American football films, *North Dallas Forty*, the impression is partly misleading, for Stone has underlined what viewers might sense unaided: his vision of the game's heroic and aesthetic aspects – 'To me there's a poetry ... as sure as Sam Peckinpah had it in his westerns, to me there's a poetry about the collisions, the helmets, the colors ... it's so beautiful.' He has also recognised the dilemmas attendant on the closures of sports films when defending having 'the fairytale... the happy ending', the 'millennial optimism', of the Sharks defeating the Dallas Knights in the playoffs, even though this denies 'a more intellectually rigorous attempt' in which the Sharks would lose, thus testing the coach's philosophy that how one wins or loses is more important than winning or losing. (Stone, Commentary Warner Bros. DVD, Special

Edition Director's Cut, material circulated in various interviews). Actually, *Any Given Sunday* slips a reversed version of the 'two endings' victory plot ('Plots and Superplots', Introduction), almost beneath viewer awareness, when the coach's farewell speech refers obliquely to San Francisco later defeating the Sharks, a notation doubly oblique in its placement in a coda among the end titles. Thus the film mixes critique with affirmation, satire with the heroic, celebrating a game remembered as once better, but still retaining virtues to be celebrated.

'The gladiators of their time'

The militaristic ethos surrounding American football is either celebrated or unflinchingly revealed, or both together, in numerous films, as in *Any Given Sunday* where the epigraph from the legendary coach Vince Lombardi is notable for its 'field of battle' imagery, and where the coach protagonist's father has been both a great footballer and an army hero, as if the two were symbiotic. In *The Longest Yard*'s admittedly extreme circumstances, the game's rationale is all but reduced to violence as prisoners and guards play not just to win, but to maim the opposition. Even in *Remember the Titans*, with its liberal interracial agenda, the black coach Herman Boone tells the boys 'This is no democracy, it's a dictatorship' and prefaces marine-style training with 'Let's go to War!' Boone (Denzel Washington), presented as a highly positive figure, bullies a boy for saying football is 'fun', an act to be understood as instilling a necessary heroic hardness inherited from Knute Rockne's masculinising philosophy. Military metaphors are common to most sports – ' attack', 'defend', 'fight', 'raid', 'hit', 'make a stand' and so on but seem more naturalised in American football than elsewhere. In *Any Given Sunday* when the Sharks score, one player even mimics machine-gunning the opposition. When coach Tony invites the new star quarter back to dinner, his television is showing the chariot race in Wyler's *Ben Hur* (1959). Noticing this, Beamen comments 'the gladiators of their time, huh?', as the race brings into allusive focus the Roman epic's lethal games, and, moving forwards as well as backwards, a minor sub-type of the sports genre, the 'dystopic future sports film', which extrapolates from the heaviest contact sports new 'games' whose primary rationale is violence – whether the contemporary free-for-all of roller gaming (*Kansas City Bomber,* Jerrold Freeman, 1972), or the perverse Russian roulette competitions staged for gambler-

Bread and circuses in *Rollerball*

voyeurs in *Tzameti 13*, or, projected into a future where the corporation-ruled masses are entertained by deadly contests, *Death Race 2000* (Paul Bartel), and *Rollerball* (Norman Jewison, both 1975). Such comparisons may seem less extreme in the light of revelations of the frightening number of brain injuries suffered by American footballers, culminating in the 2013 AFL payment of $735 million to 4,500 litigation-threatening ex-players. But the presence of the ultra-violent chariot race encourages them, and Stone's celebration of the game's aesthetics invokes the violence of Peckinpah's cinema. If the sporting contest can be American football films than in those of other sports (except boxing), and even less in Stone's film than in others of the sub-type.

The coach

Although *Any Given Sunday* is notable for its extensive cast of characters, producing an illusion of the wider institution's totality, its primary focus is Tony D'Amato (Al Pacino), the Miami Sharks' coach. This underlines its contemporaneity, since the coach is arguably the recent sports film's defining figure. Others with coach protagonists include *Coach Carter*, *Hoosiers*, *Remember the Titans*, *The Miracle of Oxford*, *Friday Night Lights* and *The Bad News Bears* (both versions), along with instances where the coach has a major role, e.g. *Iron Ladies*, *The Club*, *Chak de India!*, *Old Scores*, *A League of Their Own*, *Chariots of Fire*, *Iqbal*, *Say Salaam India*, *The Four Minute Mile* and *Without Limits* (Robert Towne, 1998), the last two containing portraits of celebrated real life running coaches, Franz Stampfl, Percy Cerutti and Bill Bowerman. The coach's recent filmic predominance reflects modern sport's ever increasing rationalisation – a major theme of Weberian sports sociologists – nowhere more evident than in American football's different squads for offence and defence, other extremes of specialisation, and off-field control of play (but also in the influence of 'sabermetrics' on baseball celebrated in *Moneyball*, in which the General Manager hero secondarises the coach in a reversal of usual patterns). But there are other reasons for the coach's cinematic centrality. In an age where players increasingly cede decisions to others, the coach/manager becomes a dramatically potent figure, making crucial choices, bearing ultimate responsibility, and facing extreme pressures from all sides – in *Any Given Sunday* a hostile owner-manager, an unsuccessful season, absenting fans, problems with players and injuries, and a hypercritical sports media. He is also in the growingly youthful world of professional sport the man of experience and memory, of greater interior interest than those he coaches, frequently reconciling hostile parties, and often a moral mentor to his charges (the Coach Carter syndrome).

Al Pacino's Tony D'Amato is a particularly riven version of this character. His personal life sacrificed to the game, football represents for him a parallel, less-muddled world: 'The game's all that matters, because it's pure. Four quarters. You cross a line you score. It's sane. Life isn't. Life's fucked.' The film's central presence, he is a split figure, embodying the clashing values of pragmatism and idealism, instrumentalism and loyalty in contemporary sport. As ruthlessly success-driven as his competitors, he still believes the game stands for more than winning, for history and tradition, hence the photo gallery of past players in his apartment and the presence of 'ghosts', the shadowy forms of those players, vivified in his (and/or the narration's) sepia-tinted reveries. In a business-dominated, instrumentalist sporting culture, he remains loyal to the team's older stalwarts, Cap Rooney and Shark Lavay, whom the owner, Christina Pagniacci (Cameron Diaz), plans to sell, largely standing as she does, with her Forbes business magazine cover appearance, and threat to remove the team from its Miami fans to Los Angeles in her dispute with the mayor over financing a new stadium, as the antithesis of Tony's cherishing of the game. However, some of her representativeness is compromised by the unreality of blaming a female (paralleled by other equally unrepresentative destructive female owners

The classic coach and star relationship in *Any Given Sunday*

in *Slapshot* and *Major League*) for the actions of an almost wholly male run sporting industry, something difficult not to interpret in anti-feminist backlash terms (Baker 2003: 144).

In a high contact sport where medics cluster like corpsmen near the frontline, and, as in *North Dallas Forty*, getting injured bodies on the field at any cost is a corrupting priority, Christina encourages the team's chief doctor, Harvey Mandrake, to risk Shark's health by hiding evidence of his fractured neck, when an unlucky hit could kill him. Learning of Mandrake's actions, Tony immediately dismisses him, despite the medic's defence that he only does what the players want (certainly true of Shark who will take any risk to secure his million dollar bonus). Yet, when Shark pleads to play, Tony eventually agrees, subject to him signing a waiver, and later, aware of Cap's possible neurological damage, pressures him into playing a vital game. Both players make major contributions to the win, but suffer injuries which briefly look serious, even life-threatening enough to suggest dire outcomes to the coach's gambles. Tony's actions here as he wrestles with pragmatic, personal and ethical demands, are, at the least, morally questionable, underlining his role as a protagonist who embodies the tensions and contradictions of modern sport generally, exacerbated by the peculiar characteristics of American football and its enormous television revenues.

'Kiss my Armani ass'

Talking intimately with his colleague Monroe (Jim Brown), Tony condemns television's influence on the game in terms that echo Stone's views that the media time outs it has imposed for extra advertising time, have interrupted the flow of the game and stretched it to an undesirable length (Stone, DVD Commentary), 'I mean the first time they stopped the game to cut away to a fucking commercial, that was the end of it'. The economic power and imperatives of television are continually manifested in the film through the pervasive presence of screens broadcasting football games, replays, highlights, panel discussions and interviews. For instance, while Monroe and Tony are talking, a TV screen shows one of Willie's adverts, and while Tony is with the hooker, Mandy, Willie's interview with the football pundit Jack Rose is screened. Television is the most vital component of the lucrative advertising contracts that the Sharks' players have access to, but which cause problems of team unity, for instance the tension between Washington and Beamen when the new quarterback's style gives Washington fewer opportunities. His critique of Beamen's disruptions of the team are valid, but in part driven by his need for personal yardage to clinch a Reebok contract, as Tony's rebuke – 'This team isn't about your damn stats!' – indicates, underlining the constant temptation for the players to play for personally enriching 'stats' rather than for the team. Hence Tony's approving shout of 'Unselfish!' when Washington runs into touch, sacrificing individual yards to the team effort in the big playoff game, though the fact that the coach views this as notable speaks volumes about the ethos of the sport in a market-driven era in which both club and players regard each other as easily tradeable commodities. The spectacle of advertising, symbiotically connected with the spectacle of the game and the spectacle of the players' sex and drug orgies, culminates in the major sequence where Willie's Met-RX commercial is shot. As his celebrity takes off, Willie becomes the centrepiece of such advertising, creating for himself the persona of 'Steamin' Beamen', who 'keeps the women creamin', based around commodification of his black sexuality.

Coach and quarterback

The fraught relationship between coach and star, Willie Beamen (Jamie Foxx), runs through the film, intersecting many of its concerns. The third choice quarterback, given his chance through injuries, Beamen is immediately acclaimed by tele-journalists and commentators for his brilliant running. However, his improvised overriding of Tony's playbook calls brings the

The sportsman as commodity in *Any Given Sunday*

two into conflict, exacerbated by their many differences – of age, colour, outlook and style – centred around team versus individual, planning versus intuition, intellect versus gut feeling, tradition versus innovation. Though the coach's subjectivity has narrative priority, the film enacts no absolute alignment with either side of the argument, since neither set of values can exist in isolation from the other in a team sport. Though the racial difference is fundamental, it is nevertheless simplistic to see the conflict only in terms of black values against the white bourgeois 'masculine self-reliance' that has been too simply identified as the film's ideology (see Baker 2003: 142–47), despite Tony emphasising teamwork above all, and Beamen individualist self-assertion. Like the coach, the star player is a contradictory figure, the product of the contemporary as distinct from the traditional game, capable of trenchant insight in his criticisms of the lack of black management and coaches, but at the same time self destructively insulting black teammates with fabricated black power rhetoric, shown to be opportunistic when he asks Christina out, and badmouthing their playing ability to the point that Julian Washington threatens him, Shark Lavay destroys his car, and in the New York Emperors game he is continually sacked because his colleagues refuse to protect him. In a classic compromise enacted in the narrative's last movements both Beamen and D'Amato move away from their fixed positions, with Beamen admiring and learning from Cap Rooney, and, when he replaces him, apologising to his team mates, while Tony gives the quarterback free rein in the game's last moments where Beamen apparently has a vision of one of the 'ghosts' he has previously discounted, which inspires him to his brilliant winning play. Tony's farewell speech announces that he is moving to the Arizona Aztecs and taking Willie with him, which suggests that both have an ongoing future in a new team in which their differences will be creative rather than destructive.

An auteurist sports film

Regardless of deeply conflicting estimates of his work, Stone's claim to auteurship is indisputable. His only sports film exhibits thematic concerns deeply embedded in his oeuvre – a double-edged fascination with corporate America; an equally double-edged obsession with war, with the close range football sequences emphasising violent collision, the hits sonically augmented as in the contemporary war film; as well as a trademark attraction to excess: a player snorting cocaine from a groupie's breast, a baby alligator loosed in the showers, the theatre of cruelty spectacle of a player's eye popping out ('out vile jelly') to be rescued and ice -packed by paramedics. With its estimated 3,200 shots (even more than *Natural Born Killers*' approximately 3,000), *Any Given Sunday* abounds in extremely rapid montage and a barrage of flash-pans, superimpositions, interpolated shots, camera movements as much for sensation as information and deliberate confusion between characters' subjective views and authorial rhetoric. Stone's dominant strategies may be simplified to two techniques: (i) associative editing generating conceptual meanings, e.g. the single interpolated shot, before the big party sequence, of the earth viewed from space, interpretable as a communications satellite's view of its territory in a media-dominated narrative; (ii) a barrage of devices creating both on- and off-field excitation – though a question, beyond the remit of this analysis, is whether (ii) compromises (i), something denied by Stone's argument that his work's 'vast Promethean energy' demands extreme quickness of eye and brain (Stone, DVD commentary). The film's most noted instance of conceptual editing occurs when Beamen dines at D'Amato's apartment, a scene impinged on by the moments from *Ben Hur* playing on the television, a conjunction that Stone convincingly claims produces, in addition to its gladiatorial and competitive meanings, a parallel between D'Amato and Beamen and Charlton Heston (Ben Hur) and Jack Hawkins (Quintus Arrius, the Roman commander of the slave galley), with Beamen in, or seeing himself in, Heston's role as slave, and D'Amato in Hawkins' as slavedriver/ commander, with the bonus of Heston also appearing later in the film as the Football Commissioner. In fact, a further parallel can be argued with Quintus Arrius' later adoption of Ben Hur echoing the vexed metaphorical father-son relationship of coach and star.

The larger scene in which these identifications take place is a paradigm of *Any Given Sunday*'s combination of mainstream classical narrative and flurries of rapid associative editing. The conversation between coach and player about their different conceptions of football, classical at base in its linear development and basic spatial coherence, is, however, intersected by (i) the TV showing of the chariot race and a scene on the Roman slave galley. At first, part of the background *mise-en-scène*, comparable to the glimpse of *Harvey* on TV in *Field of Dreams*, the film within the film becomes foregrounded in fullscreen closeup, enforcing the parallels to the point that Heston and Hawkins occasionally seem to be interrelating with Pacino and Foxx. The fact that the *Ben Hur* scenes are shown out of chronological order (the galley scene should precede the race) emphasises the artifice of the trope, with the generation of meaning prioritised over strict accuracy. The scene is further intersected by (ii) shots of the 'ghosts' of the past greats, Unitas, Baugh and others playing; by (iii) shots quoted from earlier in the film – e.g. the huge close up of the ball with the player's hand on it from the film's opening, a juddering tackle in the dark and rain from the New York Emperors game; and by (iv) travelling shots across the water towards other parts of the city, and repeated cuts to gathering clouds. In the most rapid montages the conversation is intersected with chariot collisions intercut with almost subliminal images of the 'ghosts' and shots from earlier in the film, with, as a driver falls from a chariot, a footballer, hit by the opposition, hurtling through the air, sequences suggestive of Soviet revolutionary montage, though stripped of the ideological and precise aesthetic imperatives of the original, the sports/competition/war equivalences here operating in a largely morally neutral sphere.

This brief concentration on Stone's stylistics in no sense asserts *Any Given Sunday* as a particular template for other sports films – both American football as a subject and Stone's stylistic procedures being particularly idiosyncratic – but suggests more generally that its combination of mainstream narrative strategies (essential to a popular genre) and stylistic innovations (at least for mainstream entertainment film) is an example of the sports film possessing a flexibility to engage with both changing actual world realities and stylistic paradigms, as it continues to be, for the foreseeable future, a productive and developing genre.

SELECT FILMOGRAPHY

8 Men Out (baseball) (US), John Sayles, 1988.

Afghan Cricket Club: *Out of the Ashes* (cricket documentary) (UK),Tim Albone, Lucy Martens, Leslie Knott, 2011.

Alex (swimming) (New Zealand), Megan Simpson, 1993.

Ali (boxing) (US), Michael Mann, 2001.

Allez France! (rugby union)(France), Robert Dhery and Pierre Tchernia, 1964.

Angels in the Outfield (baseball) (US), Clarence Brown, 1951.

Any Given Sunday (American football) (US), Oliver Stone, 1999.

Australian Rules (Australian Rules football) (Australia), Paul Goldman, 2002.

The Babe (baseball) (US), Arthur Hiller, 1992.

The Babe Ruth Story (baseball) (US), Roy Del Ruth, 1948.

Bang the Drum Slowly (baseball) (US), John D. Hancock, 1973.

The Bad News Bears (baseball) (US), Michael Ritchie, 1976.

Battling Butler (boxing), (US), Buster Keaton, 1926.

Beautiful Boxer (Muay Thai kickboxing) (Thailand), Ekachai Uekrongtham, 2003.

Bend It Like Beckham (football) (UK), Gurinder Chadha, 2003.

Best (football) (UK), Mary McGuckian, 2000.

Big Wednesday (surfing) (US), John Milius, 1978.

The Bingo Long Travelling All-Stars and Motor Kings (baseball) (US), John Badham, 1976.

Blue Crush (surfing) (US), John Stockwell, 2003.

Body and Soul (boxing) (US), Robert Rossen, 1947.

Bodyline (cricket) (Australia), Denny Lawrence *et al*, 1984 (TV mini-series).

Breaking Away (cycling) (US), Peter Yates, 1980.

Bull Durham (baseball) (US), Ron Shelton, 1988.

Caddyshack (golf) (US), Harold Ramis, 1988.

Chak De India! (hockey) (India), Shimit Amin, 2007.

Champion (boxing) (US), Mark Robson, 1949.

Champion/Hangui (boxing) (South Korea), Kyung-Taek Kwak, 2002.

Champions (horseracing) (UK) , John Irvin, 1984.

Chariots of Fire (athletics) (UK), Hugh Hudson, 1981.

Chennai 600028 (cricket) (India, Tamil language), Venkat Prabhu, 2007.

Cinderella Man (boxing) (US), Ron Howard, 2005.

City Lights (boxing scene) (US), Charles Chaplin, 1931.

The Club (Australian Rules football) (Australia), Bruce Beresford, 1980.

Coach Carter (basketball) (US), Thomas Carter, 2005.

Cobb (baseball) (US), Ron Shelton, 1994.

College (athletics) (US), James W. Horne, 1927.

The Color of Money (pool) (US), Martin Scorsese, 1986.

Cool Runnings (bobsleigh) (US), John Turteltaub, 1993.

Crying Fist/Jumeogi Unda (boxing) (South Korea), Ryu Seung-Wan, 2005.

The Cup (football) (Bhutan/Australia), Khyentse Norbu, 2000.

Damn Yankees (baseball) (US), George Abbott and Stanley Donen, 1958.

The Damned United (football) (UK), Tom Hooper, 2009.

Death Race 2000 (future sport) (US), Paul Bartel, 1975.

Dawn! (swimming) (Australia), Ken Hannam, 1979.

Downhill Racer (skiing) (US), Michael Ritchie, 1969.

Escape to Victory (football) (US), John Huston, 1981.

Excuse My Dust (motor racing) (US), Sam Wood, 1920.

The Fan (baseball) (US), Tony Scott, 1996.

Fat City (boxing) (US), John Huston, 1972.

Fear Strikes Out (baseball) (US), Robert Mulligan, 1957.

Fever Pitch (football) (UK), David Evans, 1997.

Field of Dreams (baseball) (US), Phil Alden Robinson, 1989.

Fire in Babylon (cricket documentary) (UK), Stevan Riley, 2010.

Fight Club (underground fighting) (US), David Fincher, 1999.

The Final Test (cricket) (UK), Anthony Asquith, 1953.

The Final Winter (rugby league) (Australia), Brian Andrews and Jane

Forrest, 2007.

The Firm (football hooliganism) (UK), Alan Clarke, 1988.

Follow the Sun (golf) (US), Sidney Lanfield, 1951.

The Four Minute Mile (athletics) (UK/Australia), Jim Goddard, 1988.

The Freshman (American football) (US), Harold Lloyd, 1925.

Friday Night Lights (American football)(US), Peter Berg, 2004.

From the Ashes (cricket documentary) (UK), James Erskine, 2011.

Gentleman Jim (boxing) (US), Raoul Walsh, 1942.

Geordie (hammer throwing) (UK), Frank Launder, 1956.

Girlfight (boxing) (US), Karyn Kusama, 2001.

The Goalkeeper's Fear of the Penalty/Die Angst der Tormanns beim Elfmeter (football) (West Germany), Wim Wenders, 1972.

The Go-Between (cricket scene) (UK), Joseph Losey, 1970.

Golden Boy (boxing) (US) Rouben Mamoulian, 1939.

Golden Gloves (boxing documentary) (Canada) Gilles Groulx, 1961.

The Golf Expert (golf) (US), Monte Brice, 1930.

Gracie (football) (US), Davis Guggenheim, 2007.

Grand Prix (motor racing) (US), John Frankenheimer, 1966.

The Great White Hope (boxing) (US), Martin Ritt, 1970.

Gregory's Girl (football scenes) (UK), Bill Forsyth, 1981.

Hard, Fast and Beautiful (tennis) (US), Ida Lupino, 1951.

The Harder They Fall (boxing) (US), Mark Robson, 1956.

Heart Like a Wheel (drag car racing) (US), Jonathan Kaplan, 1983.

Hoop Dreams (basketball documentary) (US), Steve James, 1994.

Hoosiers (basketball) (US), David Anspaugh, 1986.

Horse Feathers (American football scenes) (US), Norman McLeod, 1932.

The Hustler (pool) (US), Robert Rossen, 1961.

Ice Castles (figure skating) (US), Donald Wrye, 1978.

I Know How Many Runs You Scored Last Summer (cricket) (Australia), Stacey Edmonds and Doug Turner, 2008.

Iqbal (cricket) (India), Nagesh Kukunoor, 2005.

Iron Ladies/Satri Lek (volleyball) (Thailand),Youngyuth Thongonthung, 2000.

It's Not Cricket (cricket) (UK), Roy Rich, Alfred Roome, 1949.

The Jackie Robinson Story (baseball) (US), Alfred E. Green, 1950.

Jerry Maguire (sports agency) (US), Cameron Crowe, 1996.

Jim Thorpe All American (athletics, American football) (US), Michael Curtiz, 1951.

The Joe Louis Story (boxing) (US), Robert Gordon, 1953.

Kaikohe Demolition (stock car documentary) (New Zealand), Florian Habicht, 2004.

Kansas City Bomber (roller game) (US), Jerrold Freeman,1972.

The Kid From Brooklyn (boxing) (US), Norman Z.McLeod, 1946.

Knute Rockne All American (American football) (US), Lloyd Bacon, 1940.

Lagaan: Once upon a Time in India (cricket) (India), Ashutosh Gowariker, 2001.

La Gran Final (football) (Spain), Gerardo Olivares, 2006.

L'Air de Paris (boxing) (France), Marcel Carné, 1954.

Le Mans (motor racing) (US), Lee H.Katzin, 1971.

A League of Their Own (baseball) (US), Penny Marshall, 1992.

Leatherheads (American football) (US), George Clooney, 2008.

The Legend of Bagger Vance (golf) (US), Robert Redford, 2000.

Les Boys (ice hockey) (Quebec Canada), Louis Saia, 1997.

The Loneliness of the Long Distance Runner (athletics) (UK),Tony Richardson, 1962.

The Longest Yard (aka *The Mean Machine*) (American football) (US), Robert Aldrich, 1974.

Looking for Eric (football) (UK), Ken Loach, 2009.

The Main Event (boxing) (US), Howard Zieff, 1979.

Major League (baseball) (US), David S. Ward, 1999.

Mike Bassett England Manager (football) (UK), Steve Barron, 2001.

The Milky Way (boxing) (US), Leo McCarey, 1936.

Million Dollar Baby (boxing) (US), Clint Eastwood, 2004.

Miracle at Oxford (aka *True Blue*) (rowing) (UK), Ferdinand Fairfax, 1996.

The Miracle of Bern (football) (Germany), Sönke Wortmann, 2003.

Mister Baseball (baseball) (US), Fred Schepisi, 1992.

Moneyball (baseball) (US), Bennett Miller, 2011.

Movie Movie (boxing) (US), Stanley Donen, 1978.

Murderball (wheelchair rugby documentary) (US), Henry Rubin and Dana Shapiro, 2005.

La Natation par Jean Taris (swimming) (Fr), Jean Vigo, 1931.

National Velvet (horseracing) (US), Michael Curtiz, 1944.

The Natural (baseball) (US), Barry Levinson, 1984.

North Dallas Forty (American football) (US), Ted Kotcheff, 1979.

Offside (football) (Iran), Jafar Panahi, 2006.
Old Scores (rugby union) (New Zealand/Wales), Alan Clayton, 1991.
Olympia (documentary) (Germany), Leni Riefenstahl, 1938.
Once a Jolly Swagman (speedway) (UK), Jack Lee, 1949.
The One and Only (professional wrestling) (US), Carl Reiner,1978.
Pat and Mike (golf, tennis) (US), George Cukor, 1952.
Personal Best (athletics) (US), Robert Towne, 1982.
Phar Lap (horse racing) (Australia), Simon Wincer, 1983.
Ping Pong (table tennis) (Japan), Fumihiko Sori, 2002.
Playing Away (cricket) (UK), Horace Ové, 1987.
Pool Sharks (pool) (US), Edwin Middleton, 1915.
The Pride of the Yankees (baseball) (US), Sam Wood, 1942.
P'tang Yang Kipperbang (cricket) (UK), Michael Apted, 1982.
Purely Belter (football) (UK), Mark Herman, 2000.
Raging Bull (boxing) (US), Martin Scorsese, 1980.
The Rainbow Jacket (horseracing) (UK), Basil Dearden, 1954.
Remember the Titans (American football) (US), Boaz Yakin, 2000.
Requiem for a Heavyweight (boxing) (US), Ralph Nelson, 1962.
The Ring (boxing) (UK), Alfred Hitchcock, 1927.
The Roaring Road (motor racing) (US), James Cruze, 1919.
Rocky (boxing) (US), John G. Avildsen, 1976.
Rocky Balboa (boxing) (US), Sylvester Stallone, 2007.
Rocco and His Brothers/Rocco e suoi Fratelli (boxing scenes) (Italy),
    Luchino Visconti, 1960.
Rollerball (future sport) (US), Norman Jewison, 1975.
Say Salaam India (cricket) (India), Subhash Kapoor, 2007.
Seabiscuit (horseracing) (US), Gary Ross, 2003.
Seducing Dr Lewis (cricket scenes) (Quebec, Canada), Jean Francois
    Pouliot, 2003.
Senna (motor racing documentary) (UK, France, US), Asif Kapadia, 2010.
The Set-Up (boxing) (US), Robert Wise, 1949.
Slapshot (ice hockey) (US), George Roy Hill, 1977.
Soccer Mom (football) (US), Gregory McClatchy, 2008.
Somebody Up There Likes Me (boxing) (US), Robert Wise, 1956.
Sports Movie (American football) (US), David Koechner, 2007.
The Square Ring, (boxing) (UK), Basil Relph and Michael Dearden, 1953.
Stickmen (pool) (New Zealand), Hamish Rothwell, 2001.

Stumped (cricket) (India), Gaurav Pandey, 2003.

A Sunday in Hell/En Forasdag i Helvede (cycling documentary) (Denmark), Jorgen Leth, 1977.

The Swimmer (swimming) (US), Frank Perry, 1968.

Take Me Out to the Ballgame (baseball) (US), Busby Berkeley, 1949.

This Sporting Life (rugby league) (UK), Lindsay Anderson, 1963.

Tin Cup (golf) (US), Ron Shelton, 1996.

Tokyo Olympiad (documentary) (Japan), Kon Ichikawa, 1965.

Trobriand Cricket: An Ingenious Response to Colonialism (documentary) (Australia/UK) Gary Kildea and Jerry Leach, 1976.

Two Lane Blacktop (car racing) (US), Monte Hellman, 1971.

Tzameti 13 (Russian roulette) (France), Géla Babluani, 2005.

Up 'n' Under (rugby league) (UK), John Godber, 1998.

Visions of Eight (Olympic documentary) (US/West Germany), Mai Zetterling, Arthur Penn, *et al.*, 1973.

Vive Le Tour! (cycling documentary) (France), Louis Malle, 1962.

When Billie Beat Bobby (tennis) (US), Jane Anderson, 2001.

When We Were Kings (boxing documentary)(US), Leon Gast and Taylor Hackford, 1996.

White Men Can't Jump (basketball) (US), Ron Shelton, 1992.

Wimbledon (tennis) (UK), Richard Loncraine, 2004.

Without Limits (athletics) (US), Robert Towne, 1998.

Wondrous Oblivion (cricket) (UK), Paul Morrison, 2003.

The World's Fastest Indian (motorcycling) (New Zealand/US), Roger Donaldson, 2005.

The Wrestler (professional wrestling) (US), Darren Aronofsky, 2008.

Zidane: A Twentyfirst Century Portrait/Zidane, un Portrait du 21e Siècle (football) (France/Iceland), Douglas Gordon and Philippe Parreno, 2006.

SELECT BIBLIOGRAPHY

Altman, Rick (1999) *Film/Genre*. London: British Film Institute.

Anderson, Lindsay (2004) *Never Apologise: The Collected Writings*, Paul Ryan, ed. London: Plexus.

Baker, Aaron (2003) *Contesting Identities: Sports in American Film*. Chicago: University of Illinois Press.

Barr, Charles (2003) 'Sports Films', in Brian McFarlane (ed.) *The Encyclopedia of British Film*. London: British Film Institute, 630–31.

Barr, Charles (2004) '"What's Happening to England?": Twentieth Century Cricket', in Stephen Caunce, Ewa Mazierska, Susan Sydney-Smith and John K. Walton (eds) *Relocating Britishness*. Manchester: Manchester University Press, 110–25.

Bergan, Ronald (1982) *Sports in the Movies*. London: Proteus.

Blunden, Edmund (1944) *Cricket Country*. London: Collins.

Bordwell, David, Janet Staiger and Kristin Thompson (1985) *The Classical Hollywood Cinema: Film Style and Mode of Production to 1960*. London: Routledge & Kegan Paul.

Boddy, Kasia (2008) *Boxing: A Cultural History*. London: Reaktion Books.

Coakley, Jay and Eric Dunning (eds) (2000) *Handbook of Sports Studies*. London: Sage.

Custen, George F. (1992) *Biopics: How Hollywood Constructed Public History*. New Brunswick, NJ: Rutgers University Press.

Dineen, Robert and Ashling O'Connor (2009) 'Faster, Higher, Stronger, Sadder: How the Beijing Bounce Faded' (www.timesonline.co.uk/tol/sport/olympics/article5877307ece).

Gehring, Wes D. (2004) *Mr Deeds Goes to Yankee Stadium: Baseball Films in the Capra Tradition*. Jefferson, NC: McFarland.

Giulianotti, Richard (2005) *Sport: A Critical Sociology*. Cambridge: Polity Press.

Guha, Ramachandra (2002) *A Corner of a Foreign Field: The Indian History of a British Sport*. London: Picador.

Hargreaves, Jennifer (1994) *Sporting Females: Critical Issues in the History and Sociology of Women's Sports*. London: Routledge.

Hazlitt, William (1982) 'The Fight' and 'The Indian Jugglers', *William Hazlitt: Selected Writings*. London: Penguin Books, 78–97, 118–135.

Huizinga, Johan H. (1970) *Homo Ludens: A Study of the Play Elements in Culture*. London: Paladin.

Inglis, Fred (1977) *In the Name of the Game*. London: Heinemann.

James, C.L.R. (1963) *Beyond a Boundary*. London: Stanley Paul.

Jones, Glen (2005) '"Down on the Floor and Give Me Ten Sit-ups": The British Sports Feature Film', *Film and History: An Interdisciplinary Journal of Film and Television Studies*, 35.2, 29–40.

King, Richard C. and David J. Leonard (eds) (2006) *Visual Economies of/in Motion: Sport in Film*. New York: Peter Lang.

Landy, Marcia (1991) *British Genres: Cinema and Society 1930–1960*. Princeton, NJ: Princeton University Press.

Lukács, Georg (1969) *The Historical Novel*. Harmondsworth: Peregrine Books.

McKernan, Luke (1996) 'Sport and the First Films', in Christopher Williams (ed.) *Cinema: The Beginnings and the Future*. London: University of Westminster Press, 107–116.

Murray, Les (2003) *New Collected Poems*. Manchester: Carcanet Press.

Musser, Charles (1990) *The Emergence of Cinema: The American Screen to 1907*. New York: Charles Scribner's Sons.

Neale, Steve (2000) *Genre and Hollywood*. London: Routledge.

Nichols, Bill (2001) *Introduction to Documentary*. Bloomington, IN: Indiana University Press.

Oates, Joyce Carol (1987) *On Boxing*. New York: Doubleday.

Sobchack, Vivian (1997) 'Baseball in the post-American cinema, or life in the minor leagues', in Aaron Baker and Todd Boyd (eds) *Out of Bounds*. Bloomington, IN: Indiana University Press, 175–97.

Sontag, Susan (1983) 'Fascinating Fascism', *The Susan Sontag Reader*, Harmondsworth: Penguin, 305–25.

Sprawson, Charles (1992) *Haunts of the Black Masseur: The Swimmer as Hero*. London: Random House.

Stern, John (2009) 'Watcher with a Sense of Direction' (interview with Ken Loach), *Wisden Cricketer Monthly*, June, 98.

Stevens, Wallace (1954) *Collected Poems*. New York: Alfred A. Knopf.

Streibel, Dan (2008) *Fight Pictures: A History of Boxing and Early Cinema*. Berkeley, CA: University of California Press.

Thompson, Francis (2001) *The Poems of Francis Thompson*, ed. Brigid M.Boardman. London: Continuum.

Wallace, David Foster (2006) 'Federer as Religious Experience', *New York Times*, 20 August, 2006.

Whannel, Garry (2008) 'Winning and Losing Respect: Narratives of Identity in Sport Films', in Emma Poulton and Martin Roderick (eds) *Sport in Films*. London: Routledge, 93–110.

Zucker, Harvey Marc and Lawrence J. Babich (1987) *Sports Films: A Complete Reference*, Jefferson, NC: McFarland.

INDEX